Teaching the Library Research Process

Second Edition

by
Carol Collier Kuhlthau

The Scarecrow Press, Inc.
Lanham, Md., & London

First published as *Teaching the Library Research Process: A Step-by-Step Program for Secondary School Students,* The Center for Applied Research in Education, Inc.: West Nyack, NY, 1985.

Dedicated to
John S. Kuhlthau

British Library Cataloguing-in-Publication data available

Library of Congress Cataloging-in-Publication Data

Kuhlthau, Carol Collier, 1937–
    Teaching the library research process / by Carol Collier Kuhlthau.—2nd ed.
        p.   cm.
    ISBN 0-8108-2723-9 (acid-free paper)
    1. Library orientation for high school students.   2. Research—Methodology—Study and teaching (Secondary)   3. Report writing—Study and teaching (Secondary)
    Z711.2.K83   1994
    025.5′678233—dc20   94-1982

Copyright © 1994 by Carol Collier Kuhlthau
Manufactured in the United States of America

Printed on acid–free paper

ABOUT THE AUTHOR

Carol Collier Kuhlthau, M.L.S., Ed.D., has been an elementary school teacher and a school library media specialist at both the elementary and high school levels. She is on the faculty of the School of Communication, Information and Library Studies at Rutgers—The State University of New Jersey.

Dr. Kuhlthau earned her M.L.S. and Ed.D. in English Education from Rutgers University in New Brunswick. She is the author of *School Librarians's Grade-by-Grade Activities Program* and *Seeking Meaning: a Process Approach to Library and Information Services.*

ACKNOWLEDGMENTS

I thank the students who participated in the study, especially the six who volunteered for case study. Thanks to John Pember, an intelligent, perceptive teacher, whose team teaching effort contributed significantly to the development of the program, and to Professor Janet Emig, whose research on the writing process was the inspiration for this study of the library research process. Finally, many thanks to Elspeth Goodin for her critical reading of the manuscript and for her enthusiastic endorsement of the project and to Mary Jane McNally for her contribution to revising this new addition.

ABOUT *TEACHING THE LIBRARY RESEARCH PROCESS*

Teaching the Library Research Process provides a comprehensive, sequential program for taking students through the intricacies of gathering information in a library when given a research assignment. It is especially suited to library media specialists and teachers, particularly of English, social studies, and science. Each section is devoted to one of the seven stages of the library research process:

1. initiating a research assignment
2. selecting a topic
3. exploring information
4. formulating a focus
5. collecting information
6. preparing to present
7. assessing the process

SPECIAL FEATURES OF THIS BOOK

Each of the seven sections provides the library media specialist and teacher with a detailed description of a particular stage in the library research process, along with activities and worksheets to help students succeed in research. The tasks in each stage are identified, as are the thoughts and feelings students are likely to have. In addition, the roles of the teacher and the library media specialist are examined and defined as they teach students to do research in a library. Each of the section activities features:

* a descriptive title
* an introduction describing the purpose of the activity
* the amount of time required for completion
* a list of materials needed
* clear, concise directions for presenting the activity
* suggestions for variations and supplementary activities

In addition, the worksheets included for most of the activities may be easily duplicated and distributed to students as either class activities or homework assignments. For easy use, material appears in quotes to give you an idea of how to present the activity, worksheet, or assignment to your students.

All students should be exposed to the seven stages of the library research process at some point in their education. However, it is not necessary to use the entire program outlined in this book for every research assignment. Simply select those best suited to your needs.

When applying this program to any research assignment, it is important to consider two factors. First, keep in mind your students' prior experience and capabilities. Second, assess the amount of time available for helping them in the library research process. The entire program may be used with students who have done little library research, or in a whole course centered on the process. Parts of the program may be selected for guidance in research assignments in any course in the curriculum.

Once students understand the stages of the library research process, they will need less guidance in applying the techniques recommended in the activities. The amount of class time spent on the program can be reduced by briefly introducing each activity in class and assigning the worksheets for homework. Adapt the program to the requirements and limitations of your situation, and gear the activities to the needs of your students.

HOW THIS PROGRAM WAS DEVELOPED

This program is based on a study conducted by the author as twenty-seven high school students went through the library research process. These students were observed as they worked on two consecutive research assignments. From the observations, case studies were developed, taken from interviews with six of the students at various points in their research. These interviews brought out their personal perspectives about what happened as they worked.

As a result of the study, seven stages of the library research process were identified through observations, interviews, questionnaires, journals, and other devices. Then a model was developed, displaying the thoughts, feelings, and actions that the students commonly experienced during each stage.

The activities in this book were developed to assist students as they progressed through the stages of the library research process. These activities were designed to help students become more aware of their own thought processes as they learn to find information for their research topics.

Students who do not understand the library research process frequently have difficulty using libraries. They often flounder because they are unaware of both different stages of information need and ways to use the library to progress through those stages.

The students studied expressed their need for guidance in doing their research. Some felt it unfair that their teachers simply assigned research papers and gave deadlines, without preparing them for the task at hand. The students thought that it would have helped to discuss what, if anything, they found as they worked on their own, and would have felt better knowing "that everyone else was lost, too," as one student put it, and learning how to solve their research problems.

This program was based on the concept that people continually form and reform their ideas about the world through their own experiences. These ideas make up a frame of reference for meeting new situations and incorporating new information into their system of ideas, or world view. Similarly, students need to be actively engaged in their own learning by having sequential experiences.

Cognitive development was also considered in setting up this program, because children pass through various stages of development, and their capabilities are determined, to an extent, by what stage they are in currently. To perform the tasks of the library research process, students need to be in what Piaget calls the "formal operational level of cognitive development, commonly reached between ages 12 and 16." At this level, students are able to think abstractly, to generalize, and to form hypotheses. All of these abilities are essential for succeeding in the library research process.

The underlying objective of this program is to interest your students in the ideas they are developing about their topics as they do research in the library. This interest will encourage them to use library sources, both to increase their understanding and to think creatively in all their schooling and throughout their lives.

INTRODUCTION

The first edition of *Teaching the Library Research Process* was published in 1985 as a program for teaching students to do a research paper. The book recommends a process approach as a unique and effective method for guiding students in their library research that was a distinct departure from the traditional "how to" manuals and source-oriented library instruction.

A major contribution of this book is that it is based on empirical study of real students in the process of preparing real research papers assigned in real courses. Students' experiences in the library are emphasized and their own perspectives of the research process are featured. The instruction and worksheets were designed to respond directly to the problems students commonly experience in each stage of the library research process.

When this book was first published, I had completed an extensive study of high school seniors in the process of doing a research paper. I had found that the way they experienced the research process was quite different from the traditional approach. The most dramatic difference occurred at the beginning stages of an assignment when students were commonly confused, uncertain and overwhelmed. They showed a need for guidance in more exploratory and formulative strategies to open up the creative process of learning from a variety of sources of information. Many of the traditional instructional tactics were overly prescriptive and highly detailed, concentrating on the mechanics of a research paper rather than on the creative process of learning about a topic or problem. The main difference between the interventions recommended in this book and those commonly used was that traditional instruction rarely acknowledged the active constructive process of learning by students.

During the ten years since the original study of high school students, I have continued to investigate the search process. So far, five studies have been completed using both qualitative and quantitative methods and a sixth study is currently underway. The model of the search process revealed and developed in the initial study has proven to hold across populations and over time. One study surveyed the original group of students four years later. This follow-up research disclosed that as college students they had a clearer sense of the research process as a whole and an understanding that a focus or theme would emerge from the information they encountered. In another study, four of these students were interviewed after they had completed their undergraduate degrees. A fourth study compared the process as experienced by low, middle, and advanced level high school seniors. The fifth study compared the process as experienced by students in high school media centers, undergraduates in academic libraries, and public library users. Each of these studies showed that people experience a similar process when researching an extensive problem over an extended period of time. People tend to be uncertain and anxious at the beginning when their thoughts are vague and ill-defined. They become more confident and interested after they have learned more about the topic or problem and have formed a personal perspective or a focus for their research.

Teaching the Library Research Process was a direct response to the obvious need for a new approach for guiding students through a research assignment and ultimately for teaching library and information skills. The process approach, while originally designed for high school students, has been found to have wider application with students in middle and junior high as well as college and graduate students. Students at all levels can benefit from an understanding of the process of library research. In fact, the process approach has proven to be extremely helpful for people of any age who have an extensive research project which requires them to present a particular perspective of a topic. The critical element is that the person form a focused point of view from the information gathered on the topic. Formulation of this type requires considerable abstraction and may be beyond children who have not reached the formal operational stage of cognitive development, in terms used by Jean Piaget. However, children in the elementary grades can actively engage in finding out about a topic and share their new knowledge in a more general way, as an excellent preparation for focused library research in secondary school and beyond.

Since the publication of this book, librarians in media centers and in academic libraries across the United States, in Canada and in other countries have adopted the process approach for their instructional programs. A series of implementation studies has been conducted to determine the effectiveness of this approach. School library media specialists have found that a process approach opens up new ways of guiding students into deep understanding of a topic or problem. Academic librarians involved in bibliographic instructions and reference services have found that the process approach gives a new perspective to dealing with students' questions.

The library research process assumes the constructivist approach to learning which underlies the major efforts for restructuring and improving education at all levels. The model of the search process reveals the active constructive process of learning from information that involves the total person, the feelings as well as the thoughts and actions. Constructivists view learning as in individual process that engages the person in finding meaning in new information based on his or her past understandings. Learning takes place not by transmission of facts but by the active construction of new ideas. The theoretical foundations for my study of the search process are the writings and research of the major constructivists: John Dewey, Jerome Bruner and George Kelly. Psychologist Kelly's classic work on the process of construction was particularly influential in the development of a search process model which included the feelings one experiences in any constructive process.

An important component in the process approach is the partnership of librarian and teacher. The lessons and worksheets were developed for librarians and teachers working together in guiding students through the complex process of researching a topic. The lessons identify which partner in the team has major responsibility for each intervention. However, specific plans for cooperative teaching have not been prescribed for all cases, since these should be selected and developed by the partners as the need arises. In this way, the team can adapt interventions to the requirements of their unique situations.

At one point, I considered developing a manual to be given directly to students to guide them in conducting their own research process. After further reflection, I rejected the idea because a fundamental element of the process approach is that the teacher–librarian team are essential for guiding, counseling and coaching students through the process. Ultimately, the process approach builds considerable independence on the students' parts, but instances occur when even the most competent searchers need counseling in the research process, no matter how able they have become. An important concept for students to learn is when and how to ask for help.

The book is divided into seven chapters, the first six of which are devoted to the six stages of the search process. Section seven provides for student reflection and self assessment in terms of the total process after completion of the assignment. For each stage the task to be accomplished and the thoughts, actions and feelings commonly experienced by students are presented. Whenever possible students' own words have been used to illustrate firsthand descriptions of what they were thinking, how they felt, and what they did during each of the stages of a research assignment. These authentic quotations, although awkward at times, depict the thoughts and feelings underlying their actions and reveal that they needed help and guidance in the process of developing an understanding of a topic and for formulating a focused perspective.

An essential element of the process approach is the acknowledgment of those feelings associated with successive stages in the search process. An important finding in the series of studies was that initial feelings of uncertainty, confusion, and anxiety which were experienced in the early stages were eventually replaced by feelings of increased confidence and interest in the later stages. Some of the most innovative interventions were designed for the earliest stages, points at which traditional programs commonly stress the mechanics of the research paper rather than the process of learning from a variety of informational sources.

Interventions addressing the sequence of feelings were developed for the first edition of this book. Describing the full process also was found to be a critical component of the process approach. Therefore, the revised edition includes a handout for students that covers the entire search process. It should be given to students in the first stages of a research assignment, for it depicts the sequence of feelings associated with changes in thoughts and actions in the process of research that students may expect to encounter. It is my experience that it is important for students to understand the complete process before they begin.

Another critical component of the process approach and a primary task of successful library research is the formulation of a focused perspective of the topic or problem. Yet a clear explanation of this important task is missing from most traditional instructional approaches.

The interventions developed for this book have proven to be of substantial help and for the most part major revision was not needed. However, in the area of technology, media centers and libraries have changed considerably since the early 1980's when this work was originally developed. In response to these changes, standard information technology has been added where appropriate, particularly the use of computerized catalogs, indexes on CD ROM, and online databases.

In many ways, this book is more timely now than when it was first published. The ability to identlfy an information need, locate appropriate information and use information to learn, make decisions and solve problems is necessary for every person. Where the research assignment might once have been considered an academic exercise, it is now seen as essential for developing the skills of formulating a focused perspective of an issue or problem from a variety of sources of information. Knowledge of how the library, as an information source, fits into the information-rich environment is important for free access to information. Developing skill in the library research process as the information search process has taken on larger significance for each individual in the information society.

The critical question before educators is how to prepare children for living full, productive lives in an information society. John Goodlad reminds us that there are three basic charges for education in a democratic society: preparation for the workplace, preparation for citizenship, and preparation for the human conversation. The knowledge and skills required to be successful in each of these areas have changed radically in the technological, information environment.

The society in which we live and the climate in which learning takes place is amazingly dynamic. We are in the midst of an age characterized by vast amounts of information and rapid change of events. In our daily lives, we constantly experience the increase and expansion of speedily-transmitted information. In our libraries, automated catalogs and online databases have become commonplace with new technologies and software emerging constantly. Electronic networks advance one interconnected system, a massive global library, with rapid delivery from one location to another through fax and e-mail. The National Research and Education Network (NREN), a vast network of electronic systems, referred to as the "highway of the mind," is close to becoming a reality, promising increased access to information and knowledge.

As these information technologies expand access to information, major problems are surfacing. One important issue is equity. There is grave danger of greater access for those who "have" and little access for those who "have not." Education plays an important role in preparing all students for access to the "highway of the mind" by developing skills for life-long learning in an information-rich environment. These skills incorporate a knowledge of the process of library research, particularly for addressing problems that require deep understanding.

Another serious problem evident in an information-rich environment is that of overload. Information overload prompts trivialization and shallow processing and may increase, rather than decrease, uncertainty and confusion. The tendency is to skim along the surface of the novelty of the moment resulting in distraction, boredom, and a lack of deep understanding. The process approach prepares students for managing information overload by developing skill in forming a focused perspective which gives them direction for collecting only what is relevant to their central purpose.

What skills do children need for succeeding in a dynamic environment of vast amounts of information and rapid change of events? Placing this question within the context of the three charges of education mentioned above, we note a critical need for skills which prepare students for the process of learning from information. Participation in the automated workplace calls for abstract thinking and critical judgments made from computer-generated information. Participation in the democratic process calls for the ability to formulate a personal perspective or point of view from a variety of electronically transmitted sources and opinions. Participation in the human conversation calls for a sense of what it means to be human and for deep understanding of the problems and opportunities before us.

How do we prepare children for living full, productive lives in an information society? Essential information processing skills are developed when students become involved in engaging problems, explore for a focused perspective, collect information to define and extend a focus, and present their focused perspective to an interested audience. The library research process approach to learning integrates subject area content with the information processing skills required for addressing real problems in real world contexts in the information age.

CONTENTS

SECTION 4   FORMING A FOCUS 79

Task of the Fourth Stage (80) • Feelings of Students While Forming a Focus (80) • Making a Decision (81) • Criteria for Forming a Focus (82) • An Aspect or a Theme? (83) • Saving Time and Effort (84) • Postponing a Focus (84) • Forming a Focus (84) • Needing to Return to a Prior Stage (85) • The Turning Point of the Research Process (86) • The "Aha" Experience (86) • Adapting and Refining a Focus (87) • Process of Forming a Focus (87) • Strategies to Form a Focus (88) • Role of the Teacher and the Library Media Specialist (89)

SECTION 5   COLLECTING INFORMATION 103

Task of the Fifth Stage (104) • Feelings of Students as They Collect Information (105) • Having a Clear Focus (105) • Making Choices (105) • Refining and Adapting the Focus (106) • Setting an Invitational Mood (107) • Increasing Interest (107) • Thinking of the Library as a Whole (107) • Searching a Library Collection (108) • Using Descriptors and Leads (108) • Understanding the Organization of Information (109) • Using the Library Catalog (109) • Using Additional Access Points (110) • Predicting the Usefulness of Sources (111) • Directed Reading (112) • Notetaking (112) • Keeping Track of Sources (113) • Role of the Teacher (113) • Role of the Library Media Specialist (114)

SECTION 6   PREPARING TO PRESENT **143**

Task of the Sixth Stage (144) • Feelings of Students While Preparing to Present (144) • Completing Library Research (145) • Keeping Within the Time Frame (145) • Exhausing Resources (146) • Making a Sufficient Effort (146) • Making a Final Check of the Library (146) • Adequately Supporting the Focus (147) • Organizing the Notes (147) • Outlining (148) • Quoting, Paraphrasing, and Summarizing (148) • Connecting and Extending (148) • Writing the Paper (149) • Footnotes (150) • Bibliography (150) • Role of the Teacher (151) • Role of the Library Media Specialist (151)

SECTION 7   ASSESSING THE PROCESS. **171**

Task of the Seventh Stage (172) • Feelings of Students After the Research Process (172) • Increasing Self-Awareness (173) • Evidence of a Focus (173) • Use of Time (174) • Use of Sources (175) • Use of the Library Media Specialist (175) • Techniques for Assessing the Research Process (176) • Time Line (176) • Flow Chart (177) • Conferences (177) • Writing a Summary Statement (177) • Role of the Teacher (178) • Role of the Library Media Specialist (178)

STAGES OF THE
LIBRARY RESEARCH PROCESS:

Section 1
Initiating a Research Assignment

TASK	To prepare for the decision of selecting a topic.
THOUGHTS	Contemplate assignment • Comprehend task • Relate prior experience and learning • Consider possible topics.
FEELINGS	Apprehension of work ahead • Uncertainty.
ACTIONS	Talk with others • Browse library collection • Write questions about prospective topics.
STRATEGIES	Brainstorm • Discuss • Contemplate possible topics • Tolerate uncertainty.

SECTION 1

Initiating a Research Assignment

TASK OF THE FIRST STAGE

The students' task in the first stage of the research process is to get ready to select a topic. First, they need to understand what is expected of them. What are the requirements of the assignment? The amount of experience that students have had with research affects the ways in which they approach the research task before them. More experienced students immediately try to establish the boundaries of the assignment. Students with little prior research experience may delay this initial task. Thus, clearly defining the requirements of the assignment must be done first in the research process and should be addressed as soon as the assignment is announced.

Students will need to be alert and attentive, assuming a receptive attitude. They are likely to ask numerous questions about the specific details of the assignment, such as "How many pages should the paper be?" "How many sources should I use?" and "How many footnotes do I need?" These specifics are difficult to standardize but you might want to set minimums to aid students in establishing the scope of their research. They need to learn that, to a certain extent, the topic determines the amount of information needed and the complexity of the library research. Some topics can be satisfactorily explored using only a few sources and explained in a few pages, while others need many sources consulted to be fully examined and will require many pages to explain.

Students must also consider how they can fulfill the requirements of the assignment. What interests them within the scope of the assignment? They must understand the assignment and consider possible topics for research.

Reacting to a Research Assignment

When a teacher assigns a research paper, the students' first and most common reaction is a feeling of apprehension and uncertainty. Some students have described their feelings in the following ways: "It's like a spontaneous kind of fear that comes over me." "I feel depressed and bogged down." "I feel overwhelmed at the amount of work ahead of me." These feelings need to be acknowledged by the teacher and the library media specialist. Students need reassurance and some methods to manage their uncertainty at this stage.

Experiencing the Library Research Process

For the student, learning the process of seeking information is as important as expanding understanding of subject matter. The library research process consists of forming ideas through information as it is located. The ideas generated in a library search lead to the need for further information, continued until the search is concluded. Although students may forget many of the facts gathered in a library search, the concepts and skills of information gathering can stay with them to offer success and enrichment to their lives long after the assignment has been completed. Understanding the library research process enables students to transfer skills to other information gathering situations.

An excellent way of helping students to learn how to research is to make them aware of the process they are entering when the research assignment is announced. They need to become more conscious of their own thoughts and feelings as they progress through the library research process. Through self-awareness, they can learn to anticipate the reactions they will have during the process. They can then begin systematically to work through the stages of the process and more confidently overcome the difficulties that they encounter.

Creating an Information Need

In an ideal situation, people begin to search for information because they want to know more about something interesting or troubling. In such cases, the motivation to seek information arises naturally out of the person's own experience. The urge to know more about something and the sense that some significant information is missing is called an information need. In an information-based society, such as ours, students must become aware of their own information needs and learn ways to fill their own information gaps.

One of the major purposes of research assignments is to create situations where students need information so that they learn how to fill the information gaps they encounter in their lives. Assigned research should be planned to enable students to increase their knowledge of a subject while they become proficient at locating and interpreting information. An additional underlying purpose of research assignments is to lead students to recognize the need for information in their own lives.

The many-layered objectives of research assignments are not always clear to students. When assigning library research, teachers often emphasize the technical aspects of the research paper, such as footnotes and bibliography, but neglect the process that students will experience during their search for information. Most research assignments give primary attention to the content of the finished product, the research paper. While the finished product is important, of course, the process of researching needs to be given equal attention at the secondary level.

Providing an Audience for Research

The traditional audience for a research paper is the teacher who makes the assignment. By broadening the audience, students' interest in library research can be heightened. The purpose of library research becomes clearer when students know that other people will be hearing about the outcome of their work.

Possibilities for sharing the outcome of students' research are numerous. Teachers can offer opportunities for sharing research findings in class. Students' research papers can be made available in the media center for others to read. Lists of titles can be noted in the school newspaper along with abstracts of the papers. A research symposium could be planned, where students share their research with faculty and other interested students. Library research competition might be held at district and state levels calling for papers commemorating special occasions or themes such as Law Day or Black History Month. Civic organizations and businesses could be asked to hold contests on subjects of special concern to them. Students should be encouraged to keep a portfolio of their library research projects to refer to and to build on in the future. They also can be encouraged to donate copies of articles they have collected from newspapers, magazines, and pamphlets for the vertical file so other students can benefit from their research.

One student described the broad audience for her library research and her desire for an even wider audience: "Sometimes you just feel a sense of accomplishment because you really like what you have written. Very often I reread my death penalty paper. A lot of people have read that paper. I used it in our Model Congress session as a basis for my argument. A lot of teachers have read it. Personally, I'd like to do something about it, like speak to our Governor, since I am so opposed to it and I did so much research on it. Sometimes it annoys me that it is just sitting at home in a drawer not doing anything."

Many opportunities exist for broadening the audience of student library research. When teachers and library media specialists are aware of the need for a wider audience and take advantage of existing opportunities as well as creating new ones, research assignments can take on new meaning and purpose for students.

Providing a Context for Research

Subject matter content is necessary, of course, to provide the essential context for library research. A library search without a topic is nothing more than an empty exercise. Successful research assignments combine subject with search and product with process. Neither can be overlooked for the most meaningful, lasting learning to take place.

Research assignments can be planned to evolve from the content of the course. A useful method for generating course-related research topics is to announce the research assignments at the beginning of the course so students can note potential research topics in class sessions and assigned readings. Also, as the course progresses, the teacher can highlight possible topics for further investigation. Several of the activities in this chapter help students to generate course-related research topics.

Designing a Research Assignment

Designing a research assignment is a challenge for even the most experienced teacher. A successful assignment creates an information need that motivates students to search in a library collection. Although this is a difficult task, there are some basic criteria for designing meaningful research assignments.

Three Elements in Research Assignments

Three elements are necessary in all research assignments. First, there should be a question or topic requiring information not available in the course textbook. Second, it should be necessary for students to search for information in an organized library collection. Third, the findings of the information search must be presented.

The first element of a research assignment is that the question raised cannot be thoroughly investigated and resolved within the confines of the curriculum materials. When an assigned essay on *Romeo and Juliet* calls for personal reactions and interpretations, it is not a research assignment, but when the assignment requires that the students seek interpretations of critics or background information not included in the text, it is a research assignment. A research assignment takes students into sources that extend and elaborate classroom learning.

The second element of a research assignment requires that students use an organized collection of information such as is found in the media center or other library. Students may gather information through observations and interviews, but for the assignment to be considered library research, they must use information gathered from an organized collection of library materials.

Occasionally, a student will locate information from a private source, such as obtaining a book from a parent or having a teacher give him or her a magazine article. Building an entire research assignment around such random sources would be unfair to students. A research assignment should be designed so that students can locate most, if not all, of their information in an organized library collection with access to additional sources through a library network.

The third element of a research assignment is the requirement that there be a presentation of the findings. The research paper is the most common means of presenting library research findings. A research paper, sometimes called a term paper, may be assigned in any subject area of the curriculum. It is a written compilation of information gathered from various sources organized to describe a chosen focus or point of view. The point of view or focus is often called a thesis statement and is the key to differentiating a research paper from a report. A research paper follows a specific format as described in a standard style manual. (A list of style manuals is given at the end of Chapter 3.)

Research does not necessarily culminate in the writing and submission of a research paper. There are numerous types of presentation ranging from informal to formal and simple to complex. The findings of library research can be presented in oral form, such as debates or discussions. Findings may be presented in visual form, such as posters, bulletin boards, models, or dioramas; or in audiovisual formats, such as photographic essays, slide shows, videotapes, and films.

Students may experience the research process in all research assignments including those resulting in less complex presentations. However, the research paper or term paper assignment usually assures that students will need to work through the full library research process.

This book presents the full research process as experienced in the assignment of a research paper. The full library research process involves initiating an assignment, selecting a topic, exploring for a focus, forming a focus, collecting information on the focus, presenting the information, and assessing the outcome.

Structure in Research Assignments

There is great variation in the way research assignments can be structured. Research assignments can be formal or casual, with ranges in between. Formal research assignments have explicit, detailed requirements. A formal assignment requires gathering information over an extended period of time and making a written presentation with bibliographic citations. A casual research assignment may be completed in a single visit to a library and is often presented orally. In making a casual assignment the teacher might say, "Check the media center to find out more about this for tomorrow's class discussion."

The degree of structure in an assignment is indicated by the amount of direction given by the teacher. Research assignments can be highly structured or quite loosely structured. Highly structured assignments direct students to investigate specific topics within distinct guidelines. To illustrate degrees of structure in assignments, consider the various ways students arrive at research topics. In a highly structured assignment, each student might be assigned a particular topic to research. In less structured research assignments, students might be given a list of alternatives from which to choose. In loosely structured assignments students might select research topics entirely on their own. Structure also is evident in the directions given on such details as the number and type of sources to be used, the mode of bibliographic citation, the format of the presentation, or numerous other specifications.

Students need a variety of types of research assignments. The combination of formal and casual assignments helps students to recognize variety in their own need for information. The casual assignment resembles the spontaneous, everyday need for information that occurs in the life of each student. The more formal assignment, which leads students through the progressive steps of gleaning and synthesizing ideas from the information in different sources, is more akin to academic or job-related research.

Experience with both highly-structured and loosely-structured research assignments and various degrees in between helps students become aware of and respond to a range of information needs. In designing a research assignment, the more important preliminary questions to ask are: How formal or casual is the assignment to be? How much structure and direction will be given to students? What other research assignments are students receiving?

Motivation and Student interest

One of the key considerations in designing a research task is motivation of students. The use of evaluation and grades to motivate students to research cannot be entirely ignored, but there are also internal motivational factors that need to be considered. How can an assignment be made to capture the interest of students so that they will want to pursue the task?

On the surface, this may seem a simple question. Generally, students are motivated by things that hold some personal interest and meaning. Therefore, it seems likely that if students are free to choose any topic that is interesting to them, they should be duly motivated; in other words, the less structure the better. In practice, however, motivating students to research is not nearly so simple. Highly structured assignments sometimes catch students' personal interest while less structured assignments can leave them floundering. Students rarely all react alike to a given assignment. An individual student may meet the same assignment with varying degrees of interest at different times.

Students learn by building on what they already know. Their use of prior learning as a basis for library research can be quite subtle; they might seem to be choosing something they know nothing about. Upon closer examination, personally selected topics have an origin in former knowledge, no matter how vague or erroneous the knowledge may be.

The issue of motivation seems to center on whether students attempt to relate the assignment to a personal information need or whether they merely interpret the assignment as something that must be done to fulfill a requirement but that holds no real personal meaning.

The most successful and meaningful research assignments are those in which students choose something that captures their interest.

Characteristics of Learners

The characteristics of students must be considered in designing a research assignment; their ability and experience must be taken into consideration. Research assignments should not be reserved for high-ability students; all students can and should be given assignments to gather information. Research assignments need to be tailored, however, to the ability, experience, and interest of particular students. For example, a research assignment for students with little past research experience and few reference skills might be to locate three magazine articles on a particular event through an index, such as *Readers' Guide to Periodical Literature* or *Infotrac,* to read the articles carefully, and to be prepared to tell the main point of each article. In another assignment, students might list information that is the same and information that is different in each article.

Announcing the Assignment: An Invitation to Research

A research assignment should have an invitation inherent within it and should be announced in an invitational tone. The invitation in a research assignment offers alternatives from which students may choose and encourages them to begin to visualize research possibilities and to anticipate exploring a number of different choices.

At the beginning of library research, students should expect to learn something new rather than merely seek to meet the requirements laid down by the teacher. Students who sense an invitational mood in library research want to learn and are willing to search for information to help them learn.

The absence of an invitational mood is apparent in a lack of interest, resistance, resignation, and impatience on the part of the students. It may not be possible to maintain the invitational mood throughout the entire library research process as there are natural lows and highs in some of the stages. However, it is important to establish such a mood at the outset of a research assignment.

The tone set when the assignment is announced strongly influences the mood students assume in the research task. For example, a teacher who gives a detailed description of the technical aspects of footnoting and bibliographic citation when announcing a research assignment tends to divert students' attention away from the challenge and intrigue of information seeking. When a library media specialist describes all of the sources that might possibly pertain to the assignment, it has a similar effect. Such details should be introduced at the proper stage in the library research process.

Every research assignment should offer an opportunity for students to choose topics that hold some personal interest. This does not mean that all assignments need to be loosely structured, but within each research assignment, there should be something to attract the interest of individual students.

At the initiation of a research assignment, students should be urged to consider what they have already learned and what has previously captured their interest in the subject matter of the related course. They should be encouraged to take their learning further and to build on what they already know. Sample assignments in three different subject areas are included in the activity section of this chapter. The assignments are designed to allow students to select an area of personal interest for library research within the subject matter of the course.

It is important for students to be aware that their ideas and thoughts will develop through the research process. Many of their ideas and thoughts are highly individual, so two people are likely to come up with quite different perspectives on the same topic. Encourage students to be open in their thinking at this stage; they should be considering as many possibilities as they can think of. Explain that the development of ideas takes time and that good ideas evolve through thinking, reflecting, investigating, discussing, and deciding. Many students hold the false expectation that the perfect topic will immediately flash into mind. They become frustrated and overly concerned if this does not occur. It is natural to be apprehensive at the beginning.

One student described her difficulty in considering research topics in this way: "You are taught in sixth grade to pick your topic right away or you are given a topic and you start taking notes. I never seemed to be with the rest of the class because I always had some confusion in my head. I was still debating, is this the right idea or is that the right idea. I don't think when you first start that teachers let you be creative enough."

Students must learn to tolerate some uncertainty so that they can proceed with the task of identifying potential research topics. They need to relax and be patient with their own uncertainty and work through their ideas calmly. Ideas need nourishment and information provides the sustenance, all of which takes time.

Involving the Media Center

Traditionally, the initiation of a research assignment takes place outside the media center. The teacher, removed from the organized collection of information and the library media specialist, announces the assignment in the classroom. When the students first arrive at the media center, they are expected to have a relatively clear idea of the topics they want to research. However, a closer look at the first stage of the library research process reveals that connection with the media center collection and contact with the library media specialist benefit students in selecting workable research topics.

When the media center is involved at the invitation of a research assignment, students are more likely to think of the assignment in relation to the organized collection of information. As they prepare to select their topics, they tend to consider the variety of sources of information as well as the limitation of the information available to them. They begin to frame their research questions in terms of what can be researched in an organized collection. For example, students can avoid the frustration of choosing topics that are too personalized or particularized, such as "the meaning of my dream." They can also avoid sweeping or global topics such as psychology or World War II, which are far too broad even for an initial general topic.

Joint Planning

When designing a research assignment, a conference with the library media specialist enables the teacher to make the assignment within the scope of the organized collection of information. In many cases, the teacher making the assignment may be unfamiliar with the source of information that relate to the assignment. A teacher need not know all of the specific sources of information pertaining to an assignment, but an awareness of the complexity of the task that he or she is assigning is essential. The teacher, as the subject matter expert, determines what material will be covered in the research assignment. The library media specialist then becomes a valuable member of the teaching team, having knowledge of specific sources that relate to the assignment, expertise in what has caused students difficulty in the past, and understanding of the way information is organized and accessed.

Once the plan of an assignment has been determined, realistic expectations can be gauged. Students can then be advised that an assignment may be difficult; they can be reassured and given helpful suggestions. To present a complex assignment as easy or to imply that only a fool would be at a loss is unfair and misleading. When research assignments are made within the perspective of a network of organized collections, students' expectations are more realistic.

Every library media specialist has experienced the frustration of having an assignment made without his or her prior knowledge. The students descend upon the media center with unrealistic expectations and a lack of preparation, and usually leave disappointed. The library media specialist needs to be involved in the formulation of the research assignment to assure a true team-teaching approach from the very start.

In the initiation stage of the library research process the objective is to enable students to prepare for the task of selecting a topic by thinking through a research assignment in terms of the organization of information in a library collection. The following activities guide students through the initiation stage by offering ways to generate research topics and to understand the library research process.

ACTIVITY 1-1
AN INVITATION TO RESEARCH

The purpose of this activity is to initiate a research assignment in an invitational tone. It prepares students to choose topics that are of personal interest from the content of the course.

Time: one 20- to 30-minute session; several brief announcements at least one to three months in advance of the assignment

Conducted by: the teacher, with the library media specialist involved in planning the assignment

Materials: handout for the research assignment (See "Preparation" for samples), two worksheets

Preparation: Prepare a handout to distribute to each student describing the assignment. See the Biology Sample 1-1A (courtesy of Shirley Read of East Brunswick [New Jersey] High School), English 1-1B (courtesy of John B. Pember of East Brunswick [New Jersey] High School), and U.S. History (1-1C) sheets at the end of this activity. It is helpful to offer a list of options from which students may choose. Avoid details about the technical aspects of the paper, such as footnoting and the form of bibliographic citation, which will be introduced later in the research process. Instead, center students' attention on generating prospective topics that can be investigated through library research.

Note: Announce the assignment in both written and oral forms. The written instructions provide students with directions that can be referred to and reflected upon during and after the class session.

Activity Directions: Advance announcements—at the beginning of the course, announce that a research paper will be one of the course requirements. Suggest that students watch for topics in their reading and in class sessions that they would like to know more about. Suggest that they identify possible topics in the margin of the notes they take in class and notes of their readings. Recommend that they keep a list of prospective topics in their notebooks. As the course progresses, call students' attention to possible research topics that are encountered in the course of study. Explain that possible research topics are those that are introduced in the text or in class discussion but could be more fully examined through library research. For example, when reading Emerson, you could suggest that Brook Farm would be an interesting topic, or in the study of the abolitionist movement, you might recommend further investigation of Garrison. Also alert students to be aware of possible research topics from current media such as newspapers, magazines, television, and radio. Distribute copies of the "Listing Possible Research topics" worksheet 1 and worksheet 2, "Generating Ideas for a Research Topic" at this time.

Research Assignment: On the day that you choose to assign the library research paper, distribute the handout describing the assignment (see the three samples). Announce the due date, allowing approximately four to six weeks for the completion of the library research and the writing of the paper. Read the assignment sheet aloud. Provide an opportunity for students to ask questions to clarify the assignment. Minimize questions that dwell on the technical aspects of the paper. For example, postpone detailed answers to questions of footnoting, bibliography, notetaking, and outlining by explaining that these will be thoroughly described as they are needed in the library research process. Highlight questions that center on consideration of possible topics for research.

Explain that their first task is to think of possible research topics. Provide time for students to survey their notes and review any lists of prospective topics they have compiled. If you choose to give a list of recommended topics, have students look over the list and check several topics that are of interest to them.

The following exercise may be used to generate research topics from the subject matter of a course. The directions stimulate ideas and center thinking on identifying possible research topics. You may say:

> "1. Think back on what we have studied in the course. Write several things that immediately come to mind.
>
> 2. Skim your textbook and any notes that you have taken for information about these topics. Carefully reread the relevant passages.
>
> 3. Think of questions that you cannot answer without further investigation."

After students have gotten started on the exercise in class, they can complete it on their own.

Follow-up: Go to Activity 1-2, "Brainstorming and Discussing." Although research assignments will vary according to the subject matter of the course and the particular learning objectives, the invitational tone should be present at the initiation of all assignments. Adapt the directions in this topic-generating activity to fit the particular assignment you are giving.

© 1994 by Carol Collier Kuhlthau

Name _____

Date _____

BIOLOGY RESEARCH PAPER

Choose one:

1. study of a geneticist
   a. biographical information
   b. books/articles written
   c. experiments performed

2. performance and analysis of an experiment dealing with photosynthesis
   a. choose a particular scientist
   b. select an experiment performed
   c. perform the experiment, collect and record all data, and analyze the results
   d. research how this experiment has helped scientists in increasing their knowledge and understanding of photosynthesis

3. comparative analysis on the topic of the origin of life (biogenesis vs. abiogenesis)
   a. name supporters of each
   b. describe experiments performed by the supporters
   c. describe theories on the origin of life (refer to experiments and library research)

4. research on the effects of nuclear energy on the DNA molecule and future generations of humans

5. analysis of lab results dealing with blood pressure/heart rate or breathing
   a. research the effects of exercise, smoking, gender, age, etc.
   b. use lab results to substantiate your research
   c. describe ways to protect your circulatory and respiratory systems and keep them healthy

6. research the possible causes of a type of cancer
   a. choose a system and organ of the human body
   b. describe possible genetic and environmental factors that cause the cancer
   c. describe possible preventatives for the cancer

7. research into what is intelligence (inherited and/or controlled by environment)

8. an approach of your own (subject to approval)

Length: 5 to 8 + pages, plus bibliography

Sample 1–1A

Name _____

Date _____

ENGLISH RESEARCH PAPER

Choose one:

1. an in-depth study of a favorite author
   a. biographical information (focus on aspects of author's life history that relate to his/her work)
   b. discussion of books you choose to read
   c. common themes, style, etc. (use critical sources rather than your own observations for the most part so that you may come to your own conclusions)

2. a literary genre (the short story, the detective story, etc.)

3. an in-depth study of a favorite book or books (extensive use of critical analysis)

4. a literary/historical era (writings of the Great Depression, the Roaring Twenties, the Beat Generation, etc.)

5. a comparative study (authors, national literatures, etc.)

6. a study of a philosophy as seen in literature

7. an approach of your own (subject to approval)

Length: 8 to 10 + pages plus bibliography

© 1994 by Carol Collier Kuhlthau

Sample 1–1B

Name _____

Date _____

U.S. HISTORY RESEARCH PAPER

Choose one:

1. an in-depth study of an important person
    a. biographical information (keep to pertinent facts and keep brief)
    b. discussion of contributions, impact, influence, etc.

2. a study of a trend or movement (labor unions, women's suffrage, desegregation, etc.)
    a. origin
    b. development
    c. effect or outcome (use research sources rather than your own observations so that you may come to your own conclusions)

3. an in-depth study of an event (Stock Market Crash, Pullman Strike, Boston Tea Party, etc.)
    a. causes
    b. description
    c. outcome, significance and impact on history (use research sources rather than your own observations so that you may come to your own conclusions)

4. a comparative study (two sides of a controversial issue, or comparison of different people, trends, events, etc.)

5. an approach of your own (subject to approval)

Length: 5 to 8 + pages plus bibliography

© 1994 by Carol Collier Kuhlthau

LISTING POSSIBLE RESEARCH TOPICS

A research paper is one of the requirements for this course. Your research topic will build on what we are learning in class. As you read the text and participate in class instruction and discussion, keep a list of the things you would like to know more about. These are prospective research topics for you to consider when you select a topic for the library research assignment. Keep this list in a convenient place in your notebook and add possible research topics as you find them.

Topics I would like to know more about.

1. _____
_____

2. _____
_____

3. _____
_____

4. _____
_____

5. _____
_____

6. _____
_____

7. _____
_____

8. _____
_____

9. _____
_____

10. _____
_____

© 1994 by Carol Collier Kuhlthau

© 1994 by Carol Collier Kuhlthau

Name _____

Date _____

GENERATING IDEAS FOR A RESEARCH TOPIC

A. Think back on what we have studied in the course. List some topics that immediately come to mind.

   1.

   2.

   3.

   4.

   5.

B. Skim your textbook and your notes for references to the topics you have listed. Reread the information you find.

C. Think of a question for each topic that you cannot answer without further investigation. Write the questions under the topics listed above.

Worksheet 1/Activity 1–1

ACTIVITY 1-2
BRAINSTORMING AND DISCUSSING

One of the main strategies students have used to prepare for the decision of selecting topics is to talk about the assignment and to discuss possible topics. This activity provides opportunities for students to generate, clarify, and share their ideas.

Time: one 40-minute session

Conducted by: the teacher with the library media specialist

Materials: chalkboard

Preparation: Activity 1-1, "An Invitation to Research," should precede this lesson.

Activity Directions: Ask students if they have any questions about the assignment now that they have had time to reflect on it. They should have an understanding of the general task of the research assignment, but they need not be overly concerned with details at this point. Students should know:

1. How they are to select a topic.
2. The scope of the assignment, including the approximate length of the presentation.
3. How the findings are to be presented.

Conduct a brainstorming session to generate ideas about possible research topics. You could say something like this to get started: "You have had some time to think of topics that you might like to research. Let's list some of the topics that you are considering on the chalkboard:" List the topics on the chalkboard as students name them.

Have students divide into groups of four or five. Direct them to discuss topics that each is considering. Use the following guidelines:

1. Tell some things that they already know about the research topics they are considering.
2. Tell some things they would like to find out about the research topics.
3. Ask questions and offer suggestions on the topics described by the other members of the group.

Allow approximately 15 minutes for the group discussions. Move around the room to spend time with each group, offering guidance where needed.

Call the class together. Suggest that they begin to read about the topics they are considering to learn more in preparation for choosing one to research. Warn students not to select a final topic before they have done some preliminary reading in the media center, saying something like this: "We will be going to the media center with the class in a few days. Do some reading on your own between now and then. Encyclopedias are one of your best sources at this point but you might also want to check what is listed in the catalog of library holdings and in an index to current periodicals."

Follow-up: During succeeding class sessions, briefly remind students to continue thinking and reading about possible topics.

Variation: The way topics are generated for research assignments varies. Adapt Activity 1-2 to match the way you have structured the assignment and the way you want students to select topics. At this stage students should be seeking something that is interesting to them and something they have some familiarity with that they can build on.

ACTIVITY 1-3
KEEPING A JOURNAL

Writing helps students formulate their ideas. Keeping a journal during a research assignment enables students to use writing to clarify their thinking. Journals also help students become aware of the process they are experiencing in library research.

Time: 10–20 minutes in class; in addition, daily entries will be made by students outside of class

Conducted by: the teacher or the library media specialist

Materials: a spiral notebook for each student

Preparation: make copies of the "Journal Instruction Sheet" (Activity Sheet 1-3) for students to keep in the front of their journals. Students who are familiar with journal writing readily adapt to using journals to log library research. Those who have not previously kept journals will need more precise instructions.

Note: The general instructions for keeping a journal during library research remain the same for the entire research process. At each stage, however, specific instructions will be given to help students in the particular part of the process they are experiencing.

Activity Directions: Announce to students that they will keep a journal of their research progress. Tell them: "Keeping a record of your thoughts and actions as you work on a research assignment helps to clarify your thinking. This is especially helpful at the beginning of your research. It is important to write in your journal every day. There may be days when you think you have nothing to write, but once you start, your ideas are likely to flow."

The following journal writing instructions are specifically for the task initiation stage of library research. Tell your students:

"1. Briefly describe your research assignment.

2. List all possible topics you are considering.

3. Write what you already know about each of the possible topics.

4. Write some further information you have found in your initial reading about the topics.

5. List the sources you consult.

6. Write some questions about each topic.

7. Describe conversations you have had about the assignment."

You could also add, "You may also want to include your feelings about the assignment. Be as comprehensive as you can and remember to write in your journal every day." Distribute copies of the "Journal Instruction Sheet."

Follow-up: Collect the journals once a week. Write brief but helpful comments in the margins. Make these comments in an invitational tone and avoid being overly critical or directive at this point. At each stage in the process, alter the specific directions to match the task the students are working on.

JOURNAL INSTRUCTION SHEET

You will need a spiral notebook to record the progress of your library research. Set aside 10 to 15 minutes each day to write in your research journal. Date each entry. Your entries may include:

1. What are my thoughts, questions and insights about my research topic?
2. What action have I taken?
   What sources have I used?
   With whom have I talked?
   What other strategies have I used? (An example is making a list of ideas and facts.)
3. What feelings am I experiencing?
4. What do I plan to do next?

The journals will be collected periodically and returned the following day. Your journal will be considered part of the research assignment to be turned in with the finished research paper.

© 1994 by Carol Collier Kuhlthau

Activity Sheet 1–3

ACTIVITY 1-4
TIME LINE OF THE RESEARCH PROCESS

Purpose: This activity demonstrates the different stages of the library research process that students can expect to experience. All of the stages are briefly described to help students visualize the research process in its entirety.

Time: 20 minutes

Conducted by: the teacher or the library media specialist

Materials: chalkboard and handout of time line (p. 25)

Activity Directions: Explain to the students that as they gather information and think about their research topic, they will progress through different stages. Draw a line approximately two feet long across the chalkboard. Announce that the stages of the research process can be shown on a time line. Suggestions for how to describe each step follow.

    1. "First, you are given a research assignment."

receive
assignment

      |_____

(uncertainty)

    "You think about the assignment and consider several possible topics. You may feel uncertain and anxious during this time."

    2. "Then you consider the possible topics and select one to research."

receive   select
assignment topic

      |_____|_____

(uncertainty) (optimism)

    "You will probably feel somewhat relieved and possibly even pleased after you have selected your topic."

    3. "You begin to gather information and read about your general topic, looking for a possible focus."

receive   select   look for
assignment topic   possible focus

      |_____|_____|_____

(uncertainty) (optimism) (confusion)

    "As you read about your topic and begin to realize how much there is to know, you may become increasingly confused and apprehensive. You will probably waver between different aspects of the topic that you might use for your research focus. Sometimes people become discouraged and want to change their topic at this point."

4. "As the different ways to focus your topic become clearer to you, you will choose one to concentrate on in your research."

receive assignment	select topic	look for possible focus	form focus
|	|	|	|
(uncertainty)	(optimism)	(confusion)	(a sense of direction)

"You will probably feel relieved at having a clearer idea of what you are doing."

5. "Next, you gather information on your focus, taking notes and keeping a record of the sources you use."

receive assignment	select topic	look for possible focus	form focus		gather information and refine focus
|	|	|	|		|
(uncertainty)	(optimism)	(confusion)	(a sense of direction) (increasing interest)		

"Your interest is likely to increase as you read and gather information about your focus."

6. "When you have sufficient information to support your focus and the sources you check begin to repeat the information you have already gathered, you have completed your search and are ready to organize your information for presenting."

receive assignment	select topic	look for possible focus	form focus		gather information and refine focus	write paper
|	|	|	|		|	|
(uncertainty)	(optimism)	(confusion)	(a sense of direction) (increasing interest)		(satisfaction) **or** (a sense of something missing)	

"At this point, most people feel a sense of accomplishment and satisfaction. However, you might have a sense that something is missing. You may want to reopen your search or you may choose to investigate further at another time, in another research project."

Have students note where they are on the time line of the research process. "At this point you may be experiencing some confusion and be a bit anxious about the assignment. Most people feel this way. The best way to work through this stage is to identify several topics you might like to research and begin to read about those topics. Distribute copies of worksheet 1-4, "Questions to Help You Select a Topic."

Follow-up: Refer back to the time line several times while students are researching their topics. Each time, have them identify where they are in the research process and note the feelings that are common to that stage.

TIME LINE OF THE LIBRARY RESEARCH PROCESS

Stages	Receive Assignment	Select Topic	Explore for Focus	Form Focus	Collect Information	Prepare to Present
Feelings	uncertainty	optimism	confusion/ frustration/ doubt	clarity	sense of direction/ confidence	relief/ sense of satisfaction or dissatisfaction

Thoughts ambiguity ⎯⎯⎯⎯⎯⎯⟶ specificity
⎯⎯⎯⎯⎯⟶
increased interest

Actions seeking relevant information ⎯⎯⟶ seeking pertinent information

© 1994 by Carol Collier Kuhlthau

Name _____

Date _____

QUESTIONS TO HELP YOU SELECT A TOPIC

1. What topic is interesting to you?

2. What do you already know about the topic?

3. What do you want to learn about the topic?

© 1994 by Carol Collier Kuhlthau

ACTIVITY 1-5
FLOW CHART OF THE LIBRARY RESEARCH PROCESS

This activity describes the steps in a library search, beginning with the assignment of the research and ending with the writing of the research paper. The flow chart is used to help students visualize the entire process.

Time: 15 minutes

Conducted by: the teacher or the library media specialist

Materials: handout of the flow chart

Activity Directions: Explain to the students that as they work through the tasks of the research process, there are sources in the library that will be particularly helpful to them, saying something like this: "The flow chart describes the tasks you will be involved with and suggests some sources that will be useful to you."

Distribute the flow chart (Figure 1-1) to each student. Read each step on the chart. Explain that you will be helping them to use the sources as they are working through the research process step by step.

Recommend that they keep the flow chart in their journals and refer to it as they are researching their topics.

Follow-up: Remind the students to refer to the flow chart at appropriate stages in the research process.

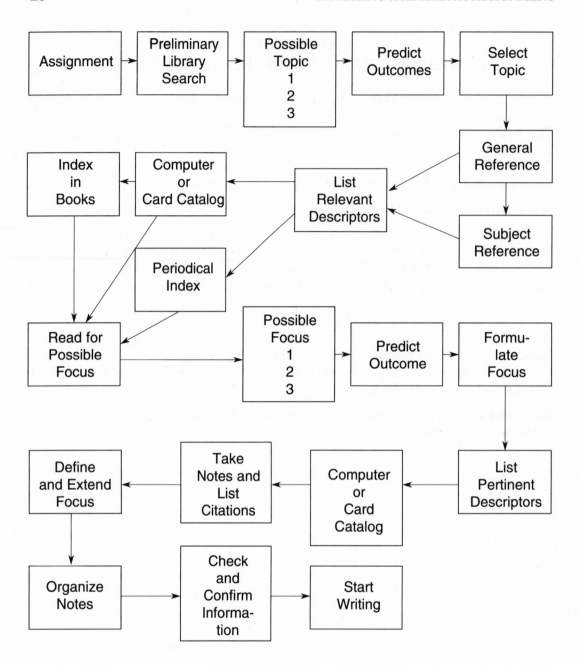

STAGES OF THE
LIBRARY RESEARCH PROCESS:

Section 2
Selecting a Topic

TASK	To decide on a topic for research.
THOUGHTS	Weigh topics against criteria of personal interest, assignment requirements, information available, and time allotted • Predict outcome of possible choices • Choose topic with potential for success.
FEELINGS	Confusion • Sometimes anxiety • Brief elation after selection • Anticipation of prospective task.
ACTIONS	Consult with others • Make preliminary search of library collection • Use encyclopedias for overview.
STRATEGIES	Discuss possible topics • Predict outcome of choices • Use general sources for overview of possible topics.

SECTION 2

Selecting a Topic

TASK OF THE SECOND STAGE

In the second stage of the research process the main task is to select a topic to research. Students need to think of some possible topics, consider each carefully, and select topics that seem best. A definite decision must be made in this stage, as a student cannot proceed further in the process without a topic to research.

Students approach decision making in different ways. They bring to the task their own past experience with selecting topics. Some students may choose a topic shortly after the assignment is announced, while others weigh their choices for some time before they definitely decide on a topic. Many have great difficulty choosing a research topic.

The task of selecting a topic should be presented as an integral phase of the research process, which requires careful consideration and time. Selecting a topic is usually presented as a preliminary act in preparation for the "real" work ahead rather than as a vital stage within the research process itself. The directions given to students at the beginning of a research assignment often imply that selecting a topic is a simple procedure that can be accomplished quickly and easily by all with little reflection, investigation, or guidance.

There are many ways to assist students in selecting topics. Encourage them to think of topics that catch their interest. Prospective topics should be based on something students know which they can build upon and extend. They can be offered activities that help them to think of topics they want to learn more about. They should be guided to investigate possible topics and to base their choice on their findings. In this stage, the task before them is to think of possible topics, consider the probable outcome of each, weigh the prospects, and choose one to research. Through guidance and assistance, new researchers can learn to perform this task more efficiently.

Feelings of Students During Topic Selection

Students are commonly confused at this stage in the research process. They are uncertain as to which topic will be the "best" one to choose. They are often unclear about exactly how to proceed, and are apprehensive about the amount of work ahead of them. These feelings of confusion and uncertainty can make students anxious about the research assignment and can actually deter their progress in selecting topics.

It is helpful for students to realize that a certain amount of confusion and indecision is to be expected. With guidance they can learn to tolerate their uncertainty and take positive steps toward deciding on research topics.

After students have selected their topics, they often experience a feeling of elation. They frequently have a spurt of enthusiasm as they anticipate the prospect of researching the topics. This feeling of elation and enthusiasm is brief and usually diminishes as they begin to encounter disconnected and sometimes conflicting information in subsequent stages of the research process.

In this early stage of the research process, it is important not to rush or unduly pressure students. Topic selection is a stage that is often summarily passed over by teachers and library media specialists in research assignments. It takes time for thoughts to develop to the point where an intelligent decision on a research topic can be made. Rushing students may force them to select topics without sufficient consideration, which can lead to difficulties later in the process. Students often settle on something to research without careful investigation and reasoning when they think everyone in the class is ahead of them.

One student explained the feeling of being behind the rest of the class: "I felt anxious when I didn't have a topic. I was upset because even though I knew the paper was due a long way off, everyone else seemed to be working and I wasn't. Then I calmed myself down."

Another student described a similar experience: "You know I had trouble finding a topic. Everyone else had one; there were only three or four of us (without a topic)."

The notion that "everyone else" has selected a topic seems to intensify the anxiety of students in the process of selecting a topic. Rather than rushing to choose a topic, most students need to be encouraged to slow down and consider possible topics carefully. A little tension moves students toward a decision, but too much tension causes anxiety that can block clear thinking and waste emotional energy that could be used for the decision-making task at hand.

Creating an Invitational Mood

Students who assume an interested attitude in the task initiation stage are in a good frame of mind for selecting topics in this second stage. They expect to learn something new in their research and are willing to investigate in order to extend what they already know. This openness is a very helpful approach to topic selection.

On the other hand, students who don't assume an air of interest tend to approach topic selection too conclusively. They seek ways to close down the research before it has begun. Sometimes, they enter the research process with preconceived notions and set ideas that they plan to support and not change with the facts they will gather from library sources. Some students seem to have a definite concept of what they will find and what they will write about even before they begin their library research.

The following example describes such a student: "Usually I don't go to the library until I have some ideas. Like one of the questions on the questionnaire was, 'A common theme evolves as I learn more about the topic.' That's definitely not true for me. Usually when a teacher suggests something, my mind says, 'This is what I'm going to do.' I get an idea almost immediately and then I research the idea, instead of researching the general thing and finding out something specific about it. I usually have that specific thing in mind. It usually doesn't change. I start out with the same topic that I end up writing a paper on. I like doing that a lot better because it throws out doing a lot of unnecessary research."

Although this student hoped to choose a topic with some personal meaning and interest, he attempted to narrow his focus before investigating the information in the library collection. He wasn't open to learning about the topic through the information he gathered. This approach to library research can cause students many problems. Rarely will they be able to find specific facts that precisely match their preconceived ideas. Since they are not open to learning from the information as they gather it, they are blind to new ideas and frequently are stalled in their information gathering and thwarted in their purpose. Rather than "throwing out a lot of unnecessary research" the approach commonly complicates the information-gathering process.

An invitational mood opens up possible choices rather than prematurely closing down the library search. The invitational mood helps students to seek to begin the investigation. Students can learn to delay closure by seeking something of interest to learn more about. They can be guided to choose topics that result in a more satisfying research process and presentation.

Making a Decision

Making a decision is the main objective of the topic selection stage. An examination of how people make decisions in general is useful for fully appreciating the complexity of the task before the students. The following is one view of decision making that is especially helpful in the process involved in selecting a research topic.

Students hold constructs or schemas they have built up through their prior experience. The ideas they have formed and the feelings associated with the ideas make up each individual's system of constructs or schema system. Their constructs form the basis for the decisions they make. When they encounter a new situation or event, they attempt to predict what will happen on the basis of what they have experienced in the past—based on their constructs. They make choices according to the outcomes they have predicted. If their predictions prove accurate, their constructs are reinforced. If their predictions prove faulty or lacking in any way, they alter their constructs to match the actual outcome. In this way, learning has taken place. Decision making is the result of making a prediction based on constructs and selecting the most appealing or appropriate outcome.

This view of decision making may be applied to the research process and particularly to the task of selecting topics. Students have thoughts and feelings or constructs about research topics that strongly influence the choices they make. They also have constructs about library research assignments, librarians, teachers, and other related things that affect the way they approach the task of selecting a topic and library research in general.

In selecting topics, students weigh the possible topics from what they already know about the topic and their constructs related to their topic. Based on their constructs about the topic and others related to library research assignments, they predict the probable outcome of their research and select topics that have the most promising outcome.

One student predicted what would happen if she chose a particular topic: "I have decided to change my topic. The other one would be too hard to find good information on."

Students select the best possible topics on the basis of their predictions of the outcome of their research. The degree of accuracy of students' predictions often determines the degree of success of their research projects. Of course, no prediction can be completely accurate in foretelling how a research topic will turn out, but guidance in making predictions can help students learn to increase the accuracy of their predictions in selecting future research topics. Faulty predictions lead students to discard workable research topics and can cause them to choose unproductive ones. One student stated just such a false, misleading prediction: "After doing some preliminary research, I found that due to the fact that F. Scott Fitzgerald is a fairly modern writer, there is not going to be enough information on this topic."

While students may have a unique frame of reference to decision making based on their own personal constructs, the basic task of this stage remains the same for all. They need to consider possible topics, weigh predicted outcomes, and select one that promises to offer success. A definite decision on a topic to research must be made in order for students to move on to the exploration stage in the research process. However, they may return to this decision if, for some reason, they find the choice has not been a good one or they encounter another topic more to their liking.

Selecting Topics that can be Defined and Extended

People continually seek ways to define and extend their constructs. Vague notions are defined for clearer meaning and ideas are extended for broader understanding, so that a person's knowledge of his or her world grows.

The purpose of researching is to define a topic more clearly and to extend former knowledge about it. Students should be encouraged to select topics they want to know more about.

The encyclopedia and dictionary are excellent sources for defining a topic. As students read an encyclopedia for an overview of a topic, they should note any unfamiliar terms. The definition of each term should be found in a dictionary. An unabridged dictionary is especially helpful for finding detailed definitions, alternative meanings, synonyms, and quotations in which the term is used.

When students are considering topics for research, they should first establish what they already know about the topic. Then they should think of some questions about the topic that spring from what they already know. Students may be encouraged to write about what they know and their related questions in their journals. The questions lead to ways the topic may be expanded. The questions become entry points for conducting an exploratory library search in the third stage of the research process.

Individual Pace in Selecting Topics

As students progress through the topic selection stage at different rates, not all of the students will be experiencing the same feeling at once. Some may be confused and anxious about their indecision while others are elated at having made a choice. The variation in the pace of students working through the task of selecting a topic needs to be considered when planning activities for a group. You will need to encourage and guide those who are attempting to select a topic, but maintain the interest of those who have chosen a topic and are ready to move on to explore their topics. Difference in pace is a recurring problem in planning activities for a group of students throughout the research process. Individual students in a group will move through the stages at different rates.

Younger, less experienced students need to adhere to a preestablished time frame that specifies when library research activities should be completed and approved. A structured time frame helps students learn to organize library research strategies sequentially. As students gain experience, they can work with fewer imposed deadlines and structure their own library research activities.

Criteria for Choosing a Topic

In making the decision to select a topic, there are four questions that students need to consider:

- Is the topic interesting to them?
- Does the topic meet the requirements of the assignment as set down by the teacher?
- Can information be gathered and organized for presentation in the time allotted?
- Is there sufficient information on the topic in the media center or in other materials available to them?

As students have more experience with research, they become more proficient at selecting topics that meet the criteria. They often need assistance in learning to apply each of the questions to their prospective topics.

Personal Interest

Students should be urged to choose topics that are personally interesting to them. They will think and read about the topic over an extended period of time and they need to select something that will sustain their interest throughout the entire library research process. One student described the importance of choosing a topic in this way: "At the beginning of a research assignment, I take a deep breath because I know the way I work and if I don't pick an interesting topic or if the topic I'm given isn't interesting, I'm not compelled to go to the library and do research. This bothers me. I feel hassled. Once I get started and I pick a topic I like, it gets a little easier."

The question of personal interest seems straightforward at first—the student finds a topic either interesting or uninteresting. But interest has several aspects that complicate the issue. First, interest changes and fluctuates with the progression of the library research. Students may be extremely interested in a topic when they first choose it. However, their interest may wane as they find conflicting and confusing information in library sources. Interest usually increases again after they choose a theme or focus for their investigation and begin to gather supportive pertinent information.

Another aspect that colors the interest issue is that students' interest is based on their past experience. We learn by building on what we know. Although students may say that they have chosen topics they know nothing about, closer study shows that the origins of most topics can be clearly traced. Students can usually explain their reasons for choosing a particular research topic. Some students described their prior acquaintance with the topics they chose to research in these ways: "I had read a little Steinbeck over the summer, so I chose Steinbeck." "When we did Albee in English in the first week of school, it was about the absurdity of life, and the teacher said 'maybe we could read Ionesco this year.' A month ago I saw it in my mom's bookcase. There were 7 or 8 plays by Ionesco and I started reading them. It's hard to read a play like that and know what it's about. I was going to read a book about him anyhow and then we had this research paper. . . ."

If students choose topics with which they truly have no past acquaintance, the task ahead will be enormous and overwhelming. They will need to familiarize themselves with the topic to form some basic constructs upon which to build further ideas. This takes time and can rarely be adequately accomplished in the period allotted for a research assignment. Inexperienced researchers sometimes make the mistake of choosing topics in which they have too little former knowledge. They need to be guided in their decisions and learn the consequences of their choices. One student described how a teacher or librarian might help: "A lot of people wish that a teacher would give them a list of 4 or 5 topics. 'Here, pick one of these.' But it's got to be something of interest. Maybe ask the student, 'What do you like or don't you like.' If it's about literature, 'What books did you read' and present the students with various points which may be expanded on.

But it's got to be something the person likes. If it isn't, it is just going to be a hassle. You are not going to get anything out of it. Just getting it out of the way, that's all."

Requirements of the Assignment

Students must carefully consider the boundaries of the assignment as set down by the teacher. What subject matter is to be covered in the research assignment? How much depth of information is expected? How extensive is the presentation to be? These questions are within the domain of the teacher and the student needs to seek a topic that will fit within the requirements set by the teacher.

Most students want to have their research topics approved by the teacher before they begin to gather information. In this way, they have the assurance that they are on the right track. Teacher's approval of topics serves two functions. First, students won't waste valuable time researching a topic that does not meet the teacher's standard only to have to change to an acceptable topic at a later time. Second, the teacher can monitor students' choices of topics to assure that they are distributed over the subject matter intended to be covered in the library research. The teacher can urge students to avoid topics that others have chosen and recommend alternate topics. Also, heavy concentration in one topic area will deplete the media center collection and make information gathering inordinately difficult for students. Of course, it is essential for the library media specialist to know the requirements of the assignment and also the topics that students are considering.

It is common practice for teachers to require students to report the research topic they have chosen and to gain approval to proceed. Instead of merely reporting a topic to the teacher, the student can have a brief conference with the teacher to discuss the proposed topic. At this time, the teacher can offer suggestions on how to proceed toward finding a focus for the research topic.

One student described seeking such recommendations at this point in the research process: "When I pick a topic on my own, I usually go to the teacher and ask for approval and see if there's any way that I can refine it." During the conference, the teacher can provide the reassurance and encouragement most students need. The student's feeling of elation and enthusiasm at having chosen a topic can be shared with the teacher. A few timely remarks such as, "That is a great idea!" or "You can find some interesting things about that!" can do much to boost a student's courage for the task ahead.

Time Allotted

The amount of time allotted for the completion of a research assignment is usually determined by the teacher and, therefore, is actually one of the requirements of the assignment. Many students give the time element such significance in deciding on one topic over another that it may be considered a separate category from the other requirements of the assignment. One student described an awareness of the time element in choosing a topic and plotting a work schedule: "I had to choose an author of a book I had already read because I didn't have that much time. I was counting the days and setting deadlines for myself. I didn't want to work on it during vacation."

An awareness of the time element enables students to select topics within realistic goals. They can establish a time frame for progressing through the stages of the research process. A total lack of concern for time may cause students to fail to pace themselves properly. A certain amount of planning and adherence to a loose schedule is useful in assuring adequate time to work through each stage. Without a sense of timing, students may find that the assignment is due before they have fully developed their topic. They may find it necessary to bring the search to a close abruptly before natural closure has been reached.

On the other hand, excessive consciousness of the limitations of time can inhibit the creativity needed to discover a topic to research. Inexperienced researchers commonly misjudge their timing. They need guidance in giving neither too much nor too little attention to the time factor throughout the research process.

The time allotted for the assignment is usually inadequate to investigate all of the interesting prospects that arise in an information search. Students need to learn to choose a focus to limit the avenues that may be explored. Other aspects of the topic must be postponed for possible investigation at another time. These unexamined avenues of research can be set aside to be drawn upon as prospective topics in future assignments.

Information Available on a Prospective Topic

A knowledge of the amount of information available on a particular topic offers the student some basis for judging how successful he or she will be in researching the topic. An overabundance of information commonly indicates that the topic is too broad. A lack of information is iikely to indicate that the topic is too narrow. Some adjustment will be necessary before a topic in either of these categories will be appropriate for library research.

One student described his consideration of the amount of information available in this way: "It sounded interesting to me and when I saw it on the list of possible research topics, I thought it would be a good topic. I thought I could develop a thesis statement. I thought there would be just enough information, not too much or too little." This student predicted that if he selected the topic, he would be successful in his research. He was as concerned with too much information as he was with too little. Not all students are as perceptive. Many benefit from guidance in ways to assess the amount of information available on a prospective topic.

To assess the information on a topic, students need to make a preliminary search of the media center collection. At this point, with only a vague notion of what they are seeking, most students have difficulty surveying the collection. They also find it difficult to formulate questions that enable others to help them.

Frequently, students either state what they want too specifically or overgeneralize their needs. They need assistance to learn how to survey available information. They also need guidance in seeking general information that will offer an overview to help them begin to formulate ideas.

Learning the difference between a preliminary search for surveying information and a comprehensive search for collecting information is essential for student researchers. Sources in a library are used for different purposes and at varying depths in the different stages of the library research process. Students can learn that making a survey of a library collection may be compared to skimming in reading. With a clear understanding of their task in this stage and a few survey techniques, students should be able to survey a library collection to assess the amount of information available in order to select a research topic.

Involving the Media Center

The media center and the expertise of the library media specialist can be of great help to students in selecting a research topic. Unfortunately, the library media specialist is rarely consulted until after the topic has been selected. The media center is usually thought of as the place to go after the student has decided on a research topic.

The media center and the library media specialist need to be involved in the process of selecting a research topic. Just as the requirements of the assignment are accepted as the domain of the teacher, the preliminary assessment of materials available is the library media specialist's domain. When the library media specialist is not involved in the task of selecting a topic, students frequently make faulty estimations of the information available and misjudge the success of their prospective topics. Many of the disappointments of new researchers could be avoided by learning from the expertise of the library media specialist. The library media specialist can advise and direct students in their preliminary investigation of the information available on a prospective topic. Students can learn to make more accurate predictions about the topics they are considering based on realistic assessments of the information available.

Conferences might be scheduled for each student to meet with the library media specialist, as were suggested with the teacher. These can take place during the same class period in which students are conferring with their teacher to have their topics approved. They can be given an opportunity first to confer with the library media specialist about the survey of materials on their prospective topics. Informal conferencing can also be offered on a more spontaneous and continuing basis. Students need to be made aware that they can consult with the library media specialist about a prospective topic by making a request at the reference desk or by signing up for an appointment, if necessary.

Students who have difficulty thinking of prospective topics may find it helpful to browse through materials in the media center. Leafing through current periodicals, reading book titles, and noting the various categories of materials, or flipping through the catalog can strike a familiar chord or spark an area of personal interest to pursue for a research topic.

Getting an Overview

The media center can be useful to students in selecting research topics in several ways. One is by providing an overview of topics under consideration so that students can base their choice on accurate and objective general information. The best source for an initial overview is a general encyclopedia. Students should acquire the habit of reading encyclopedia articles on every topic they are considering for research before they make a final decision. Occasionally, secondary students are deterred from using encyclopedias by the misconception that they are for elementary school reports or by the restriction that an encyclopedia cannot be included in the bibliography of their paper. This is unfortunate. When students start with a general encyclopedia, they acquire a basic understanding of what is generally known about the topic. At this stage, an overview is more helpful than the selected view they receive from books and periodicals. When students start with the computer or card catalog or a periodical index, they commonly find several accounts of one aspect of the topic. This selected view can be confusing and misleading at the beginning of the research process. To assist in the decision of choosing a topic, students need an overview of the general topic. Focus on a particular aspect of the topic comes later in the process.

Dictionaries, preferably unabridged, should be used to provide definitions of unfamiliar terms related to the topic that students come across in their overview reading. In addition, the definition of the general topic can offer a perspective or dimension that has not occurred to the student.

Making a Survey

Another way the media center is used during the topic selection stage is by making a survey of available materials. One of the criteria for choosing a topic is the sufficiency of the information available to the student.

Students need to get a sense of what is available in a collection but do not need to know specific titles or the location of the materials on the shelves. There are two sources that will give students a quick picture of what is available—the computer or card catalog and periodical indexes. The catalogs will alert the student to the number of books on a topic in the media center collection and the periodical index will indicate the extent of articles written on the topic. Both sources will also reveal if the topic is divided into subheadings. Surveying these sources should be sufficient to indicate if a topic is too broad or too narrow and also identify some ways that the topic may be adjusted if necessary.

In addition, the students should consult the library media specialist on the extent of other sources available. It is also a good idea for students to check whether other students are researching the same or similar topics, which might limit the availability of materials.

The library media specialist can help students clarify their ideas on prospective topics in preparation for locating general information. Library media specialists can provide accurate feedback on students' predictions about possible topics. They can also encourage and reassure students who are experiencing difficulty and guide them into a positive path toward making the decision on a topic for research.

The following activities are provided to assist students in selecting topics.

ACTIVITY 2-1
TIME LINE OF THE RESEARCH PROCESS

The time line helps students to visualize the total library research process. It enables them to visualize where they are in the process, to define the task before them, and to know what feelings to expect. The activity also helps students gain a realistic sense of timing throughout the research process.

Time: 20 minutes

Materials: chalkboard

Note: This is an extension of Activity 1-4

Conducted by: teacher or library media specialist

Activity Directions: Draw the time line of the library research process on the chalkboard, labeling the first and second stages as shown here:

```
receive          select
assignment       topic
     |             |
─────┴─────────────┴──────────────────────────────────
```

Review the first stage and briefly identify the second stage, perhaps saying, "You have received your assignment and are now preparing to select a topic." Point to the place on the time line that depicts the second stage.

Describe the Task of the Second Stage: "In the second stage of the library research process, your main task is to select a topic to research. You need to think of some possible topics, consider each carefully, and select the one that seems likely to be the best prospect for library research."

Describe the feelings that students are likely to experience in the second stage. "You may feel somewhat confused at this point; most people do. Some confusion and uncertainty is to be expected at the outset of an extensive research assignment. Once you have chosen your topic, you will feel more confident about your library research."

Follow-up: This activity is intended to be followed by activities that will lead students to select research topics they find interesting and want to learn more about.

ACTIVITY 2-2
GETTING AN OVERVIEW

Students learn to use general encyclopedias and dictionaries to get an overview of topics under consideration for research. The activity provides background information in preparation for deciding on a research topic.

Time: 30–40 minutes or one class period

Materials: general encyclopedias and unabridged dictionaries (in hard copy or on CD-ROM)

Conducted by: library media specialist with the teacher

Activity Directions: After students have identified one or more possible topics for research, they are ready to gain an overview of what is generally known about the topic. Show students where the general encyclopedias are located. Explain that general encyclopedias have relatively short articles summarizing the knowledge of subjects in most disciplines and that encyclopedias are an excellent starting point for research. Explain that there are two ways to locate information in encyclopedias: using the volume itself and studying the index. Both are arranged alphabetically. Remind students to form the habit of using both ways because the index can direct them to information on the topic that is not in the main article on the topic.

Direct students to locate and read articles on the topics they are considering, saying something like this: "Locate an article about the topic you are considering. Sit down and read the article carefully. You do not need to take notes but you do want to get an overall impression of the topic. What information is new to you? What surprises you?"

Show students where the unabridged dictionaries are located. Recommend that they look up the topics in the dictionary and read the definition carefully. You may want to say: "Note any part of the definition that is new to you. Reread it to be sure that you understand it." Encourage students to seek assistance from the library media specialist or the teacher if they are not clear on the meaning in the dictionary.

Follow-up: Urge students to continue to use encyclopedias and dictionaries for an overview of the research topics that they are considering. They should read about each topic before making their final choice. Worksheet 2-2 may be filled out for each topic the students are considering.

© 1994 by Carol Collier Kuhlthau

Name _____

Date _____

Topic _____

GETTING AN OVERVIEW

1. Locate a general encyclopedia in the media center. Write the title here.

2. Using the appropriate alphabetical volume, find an article about your topic.

   Volume _____   Pages _____

3. Read the encyclopedia article and list information that is new to you.

4. Using the index of the encyclopedia, locate information about the topic within articles on other topics.

   Volume _____   Pages _____
   _____   _____
   _____   _____

5. Read the information and list any further facts that seem important. Use the back of this worksheet if necessary.

6. Using an unabridged dictionary, find a definition for the topic. Write the definition here.

ACTIVITY 2-3
KEEPING A JOURNAL

Writing helps students to clarify ideas in preparation for selecting a topic. By stating in writing their predictions of the outcome of possible topics, students are better able to decide which topic is the best choice for research. Keeping a journal provides a record of the progress of their thinking.

Time: 30–40 minutes or one class period

Materials: spiral notebook for each student

Note: Journal writing was initiated in the first stage, in Activity 1-4. Students should be urged to continue to record their thoughts, actions, and feelings in the research process. This activity offers additional instruction designed to aid students in the task of selecting a topic.

Preparation: A copy of the activity directions may be prepared and distributed or you might read the questions for students to copy in their journals.

Activity Directions:

"1. List the possible research topics that you are considering.

2. Predict the outcome of each by answering the following questions for each topic.
   a. Will the topic hold your interest over a period of several weeks?
   b. Does the topic fit the requirements of the assignment?
   c. Is sufficient information available on the topic?
   d. Do you have adequate time to investigate the topic?"

Have the students review their answers and predict the potential success of each possible research topic.

Follow-up: Urge the students to continue to write about each topic they are considering. Worksheet 2-3 can be filled out for each possible research topic.

Name ——————————————————

Date ——————————————————

QUESTIONS TO HELP YOU SELECT A TOPIC

Possible Topic ———————————————————————————————

For each topic you are considering, answer the following questions:

1. Will the topic hold your interest over a period of several weeks?

2. Does the topic fit the requirements of the assignment?

3. Is sufficient information available on the topic?

4. Do you have adequate time to investigate the topic?

© 1994 by Carol Collier Kuhlthau

Worksheet / Activity 2–3

ACTIVITY 2-4
MAKING A SURVEY

Students learn to survey a library collection to determine the amount of information available on a topic. They will need to know the amount and type of information available to predict more accurately the outcome of their research and to select a potentially productive research topic.

Time: 30–40 minutes or one class period

Materials: The activity takes place in the media center using the computer or card catalog and a periodical index.

Conducted by: library media specialist with the teacher

Activity Directions: Explain to students that a survey of the library collection will help them to select a research topic. They can find out how much information on their topic is in the media center. Here is a suggested way to explain the task: "By checking the catalog and the index, you can tell if your topic is too broad or too narrow. If there are 20 or more titles, the topic may be too broad. If there are only one or two titles, the topic may be too narrow. The subject headings in each index may also indicate ways to limit or expand your topic."

"A survey of a library collection is like skimming in reading. You want to get an overall impression of what is available. You do not need to write the titles down or actually locate the materials. You do not need to read the materials or take notes. You do need to find out how much material is available."

The following questions help students to center on the task of surveying a library collection:

"1. What subject is the material listed under?

2. Is the topic broken down into subheadings? If so, what are they and how many are there?

3. How many titles are listed under the topic?

4. List broader subject headings that may contain information about your topic."

When students have surveyed both the catalogs and the indexes, they should have a sense of what is available on the topic in the media center.

Follow-up: After the students have completed their survey (see Worksheet 2-4) of the library collection, they should consult the library media specialist. Any misleading evidence they have gathered may be corrected before they make their final choice of a research topic.

© 1994 by Carol Collier Kuhlthau

Name _____

Date _____

Topic _____

STEPS TO SURVEY A LIBRARY COLLECTION

To get an idea about how much information is available on a topic, use two sources: the computer or card catalog and a periodical index.

1. How many titles are listed about the topic in the catalog?

2. Is the topic broken down into subheadings in the catalog? List any subheadings that you find.

3. How many articles are listed about the topic in the periodical index ?

4. Is the topic broken down into subheadings in the index? List any subheadings that you find.

5. Is the topic contained in a broader subject heading in the index? List any broader subject headings that you find.

ACTIVITY 2-5
CONFERENCING

After students have gotten an overview of their topics and made a survey of the media center collection, they should be able to predict the outcome of choosing a particular topic for research. Through conferences with the library media specialist, students can learn to interpret their findings to predict more accurately the success of a potential research topic.

Time: 10–15 minutes with each student

Conducted by: library media specialist

Materials: Conferences should take place in the media center.

Activity Directions: Schedule individual conferences with each student. (Worksheet 2-5, "Preparing for a Conference," should be distributed to the students.) Ask students to respond to the following directions:

"1. Describe an overview of your topic.

2. Describe the extent and type of materials in the media center on the topic you are considering.

3. Predict the outcome of your research if you choose the topic."

Note any false interpretations that students might have made. Recommend any further steps or retracing of steps that might be needed to gather more accurate preliminary information.

Follow-up: If students' descriptions are inadequate or inaccurate, they may need to return to the media center for further overview reading and surveying of materials.

PREPARING FOR A CONFERENCE

Before the conference, be prepared to:

1. Describe an overview of your topic.

2. Describe the extent and type of materials in the media center on the topic you are considering.

3. Predict the outcome of your research if you choose the topic.

ACTIVITY 2-6
MAKING A DECISION

Students are ready to decide on a research topic based on their preliminary investigation. In this activity they confer with the teacher on selection of a topic. The teacher approves the topic or recommends further investigation.

Time: 5–10 minutes with each student

Conducted by: teacher

Note: This activity might be incorporated in the same class period as the conferences with the library media specialist.

Activity Directions: Explain to students that they are now ready to select a research topic or perhaps have already decided on one, saying: "You have an overview of the topics you are considering. You have made a survey of library materials. You have written some of your ideas about possible topics. You have taken into consideration the amount of time that you have to complete the assignment and the requirements of the assignment. Now you need to decide on your research topic."

Have students meet with you individually to have their topics approved. (Students should bring their completed copies of Worksheet 2-6 to this conference.) If a topic is not satisfactory, make some suggestions as to how it might be altered or recommend several similar acceptable topics. Ask students to investigate the suggestions and recommendations and to consult you again when they have made their decision.

Follow-up: Give students who have not selected a topic a definite deadline for deciding and gaining your approval.

Name _____

Date _____

State the topic you have selected _____

_____

MAKING A DECISION

1. Why did you choose the topic?

2. What do you expect to find out about the topic?

3. List some sources you plan to use.

© 1994 by Carol Collier Kuhlthau

STAGES OF THE
LIBRARY RESEARCH PROCESS:

Section 3
Exploring Information

TASK	To investigate information with the intent of finding a focus.
THOUGHTS	Inability to express precise information needed • Become informed about general topic • Seek focus in information on general topic • Identify several possible focuses.
FEELINGS	Confusion • Uncertainty • Doubt • Sometimes threat.
ACTIONS	Locate relevant information • Read to become informed • List interesting facts and ideas • Make bibliographic citations.
STRATEGIES	Tolerate inconsistency and incompatibility of information encountered • Intentionally seek possible focuses • List descriptors • Read to learn about topic.

SECTION 3

Exploring Information

TASK OF THE THIRD STAGE

Once students have selected their research topics, they need to explore information on the general topic in search of a focus for their research. A focus may be one aspect of the general topic that the student chooses to concentrate on. It may be a central theme within the topic or perhaps a connecting thread between disparate bits of information about the topic.

At this point, students are often directed to narrow their topics. Narrowing a broad topic requires becoming familiar with the classification hierarchy within the subject to identify subtopics, and choosing one subtopic to focus on.

Classification hierarchy involves the bibliographic structure of a discipline, which is discussed in more detail in Chapter 5. Activity 5-5, "Understanding Classification Hierarchy," is designed to assist students in locating information through a hierarchical classification system. Although the concept of narrowing a broad topic to a more manageable subtopic is a very useful one at this stage, the process of formulating a focus for research is somewhat more complex.

The focus for research should be an aspect of the topic that students find particularly interesting and thought-provoking. It should motivate students to interpret the information they are gathering and to form some ideas and opinions of their own. A focus provides a core of meaning for the research.

A focus for research is sometimes referred to as a thesis statement. While this term does imply interpretation on the part of students, it may be overly conclusive for this stage in the research process. A thesis statement connotes a rigid, unchanging declaration. A focus, however, emerges as students explore information on their topic. The students' focus changes and develops as they read and learn more about their topic.

The task of the information exploration stage is unlike that of the prior stage, where the students could not progress in their research until they had accomplished the task of selecting a topic. Students can explore and collect information without seeking or forming a focus for their research. They can postpone or even neglect searching for a focus while proceeding with their library research. Proceeding without a focus causes difficulty for many students when they are organizing their information and writing their research papers. They often find that the information they have collected does not fit together in a logical

54

scheme. They also find that much of the information they have collected is irrelevant and not useful to them. Students need guidance to formulate a focus around which to collect and organize their information.

One student described his difficulty in writing a research paper when he did not seek a focus in his research: "I had a general idea, not a specific focus, but an idea. As I was writing I didn't know what my focus was. When I was finished, I didn't know what my focus was. My teacher says she doesn't know what my focus was. I don't think I ever acquired a focus. It was an impossible paper to write. I would just sit there and say, 'I'm stuck.' There was no outline because there was no focus and there was nothing to complete. If I learned anything from that paper it is that you have to have a focus. You have to have something to center on. You can't just have a topic. You should have an idea when you start. I had a topic but I didn't know what I wanted to do with it. I figured that when I did my research it would focus in. But I didn't let it. I kept saying this is interesting and this is interesting and I'll just smush it all together. It didn't work out."

Students should emerge from the information exploration stage ready to formulate a focus for their research. They may have more than one possible direction in which they can develop their topic. Each of the possibilities needs to be explored during this stage in preparation for the decision of forming a focus in the next stage of the research process.

Students should be directed to seek a focus after they have selected a topic. They need guidance in learning how to use library sources to identify and formulate a focus.

Feelings of Students While Exploring Information

When students first select a topic, they commonly experience a feeling of elation and are highly optimistic about the outcome of their research. As they begin to explore library materials for information about the topic, however, they rarely find precisely what they originally had in mind. They begin to experience some confusion. Different sources of information may present opposing viewpoints and conflicting perspectives. Students find bits and pieces of information that seem unconnected and inconsistent. Until some unifying thread or theme is found, the divergent and conflicting information often appears to be totally incompatible. In addition, the scope of the information on the topic may be overwhelming until one aspect has been identified for concentration. As a result, students' confusion mounts as they continue to gather information. Doubt as to the validity of the topic and their ability to perform the task may emerge. The sense of uncertainty can become quite threatening to students.

Some students expressed their feelings at this stage in the research process in this way:

"I was so confused up until the 25th. I had no idea what direction I was going in."

"I felt kind of blind because I didn't know what I was looking for."

"It seemed there was so much to do. It really scared me. It's a broad topic. I tried to narrow it down but I don't think I did that well."

Learning to Manage Feelings

Many students find this the most difficult stage in the research process. It is easy for students to become discouraged by the breadth, the inconsistency, and the incompatibility of the information they initially encounter. Learning to manage the feelings of confusion and uncertainty is important for new researchers. Some positive steps they can take toward managing their feelings are to understand that others have similar experiences and to expect and accept their feelings as a normal part of the research process.

Once students expect to be confused when they first explore their topics, they can tolerate their uncertainty. They can learn that the disquieting unpleasantness of their feelings must be endured temporarily while they gain a better understanding of the topic in general and investigate possible ways to focus their topic.

Using the time line of the research process to display the succession of feelings, students can identify where they are in the process and become aware of the feelings that are appropriate and common to that particular stage. (See Activity 3-1.)

Willingness to Learn

The attitude of students while they are gathering information in this stage is extremely important. They can easily become discouraged and annoyed with their task. They can approach the task too conclusively without the flexibility and openness to learn about their topic. An invitational mood helps students work through the task of exploring information in search of a focus.

Students who approach the task with a willingness to learn will be ready to explore possible ways to direct their research. Although students need to formulate a focus, they also need to take time to discover the options open to them. Settling on the first focus that occurs to them may close down another option that would result in more satisfying, productive research.

Requiring students to make a formal thesis statement at this point may promote premature closure. It is better to encourage students to learn about their topic by reading and reflecting on the information they gather before they decide on a focus.

One student described how she settled on the first focus she found and encountered difficulties. The student had chosen to research Hemingway's writing. In the first source she consulted, she found a reference to a code hero and decided to center her research around that idea. She later found that was one author's perspective and she could not find sufficient additional materials on it. She describes her experience this way: "The first source I used had information on the code hero, so I thought I would find the same theme in other sources but I didn't. The more I looked, the less I found."

Another student chose a focus before consulting any sources: "I mentioned something about Jane Eyre and a friend recommended the Cinderella theme in Jane Eyre. I thought that sounded like a good idea. I looked over everything but I couldn't find anything on the Cinderella theme. I was ready to tear my hair out." Both students attempted to form a focus without adequately exploring the information in the library collection.

Searching a Library Collection

The research process approach to a literature search differs significantly from the way students commonly use libraries. At the core of the process approach is the concept that students' ideas about the topic change and evolve through the information they gather. As they locate information, they are urged to read and reflect on it. The thoughts that they form through their reading leads them to seek other related information. Thinking and building ideas continue throughout the process, with students seeking more specific information as they progress through the literature search.

The emphasis in the process approach is on developing thoughts and ideas about the topic. Sources of information enable students to learn about the topic while they are gathering information rather than after the literature search has been completed. As the students read about their topics, ideas for focusing their research should begin to occur to them. After the focus has been chosen, they need to collect only that information which is directly related to the focus.

The purpose of the literature search in the exploration stage is different from the collection of information after a focus has been chosen. In a typical library search conducted by a student, the two types of searches are likely to be combined, with the unfortunate result that neither is effectively accomplished. In many cases the exploration stage is rushed through, delayed until the writing begins, or totally neglected. The information collection stage is bogged down by general material not pertinent to the focus of the research paper.

Sources in a library collection are used for different purposes in each stage of the research process. Although the same sources may be consulted repeatedly, what students are looking for changes in each stage. Their information need changes as their research progresses, as does their ability to express their need for information. In the exploration stage, students are not able to express precisely the information they are seeking. They are exploring to clarify their ideas, which will enable them to be more precise in their requests for information.

When seeking a topic in a preliminary search, students need an overview of the general topic and an estimation of the amount and type of material available. When seeking a focus in an exploratory search, students need to read to define and extend their thoughts about a topic. When gathering information on a focus in a collection search, students need specific pertinent information.

The same library sources are used for different purposes in each stage of the research process. In a preliminary search, an encyclopedia may be used to gain an overview of a general topic. In an exploratory search, an encyclopedia may be used to investigate the various aspects of the topic that might be chosen for a focus. In a collection search, an encyclopedia may be used to gather specific facts about a particular aspect of the general topic. Similarly, a periodical index may be used for a different purpose in each type of literature search. In a preliminary search, the *Readers' Guide* indicates the number of articles written on a general topic. In an exploratory search, the *Readers' Guide* reveals the various aspects of the topic on which articles have been written. In a collection search, the *Readers' Guide* directs students to specific articles that relate to their particular research focus.

Thinking of the Library as a Whole

Students need to consider the library collection as a whole rather than as a place with a few books on many topics. They need to learn to think of the entire library as an information source with a variety of materials organized to provide easy access. They need to ask how each type of source might inform them about their topic. Students who understand that the library has many different collections, such as reference, nonfiction, fiction, biography, magazines, newspapers, pamphlets, and audio-visuals can learn to approach a library search from a number of different points of access. They are prepared to make a complete literature search of many different types of information rather than settling for a few books quickly located through the computer or card catalog. They need to learn to use indexes to access materials in a network using inter-library loan or other reciprocal borrowing arrangements, in addition to using the catalog.

The librarian may also be considered an information source and a means of access to information. Students need to learn when to ask for assistance and how to express their information needs. They should learn never to leave a library without the material they are seeking before they have first consulted a librarian. A librarian can often detect a problem in a person's literature search and offer advice and direction that may lead to the needed information.

Identifying Descriptors

Information in a library collection is organized by type of material, subject, time period, and geographical location. Before using the catalog, students should be directed to find out about their topic in an encyclopedia and in a dictionary. They need to identify the who, what, when, and where in relation to their topic. The answers become descriptors that can be used as subject headings when the students are ready to search the computer or card catalog, the periodical indexes, indexes in books, and other access tools.

An encyclopedia is an excellent source of descriptors. As students read encyclopedia articles, they should note dates and places mentioned. Names of people who have contributed to the subject or are in some way involved with the topic are also helpful leads. When students have listed some descriptors of their topic, they are prepared to conduct a more comprehensive search of a library collection.

Exploring for Ideas

When a class of students comes to the media center after being given a research assignment, there is a familiar pattern of behavior. General confusion, commotion, and clamor prevail, with everyone asking for direction and demanding materials at once. The media specialist is in the middle of the commotion, attempting to provide assistance that meets the needs of each student as quickly as possible. Suddenly the bell rings to signal the end of the class period. The students exit with whatever materials they have found. The media specialist breathes a sigh of relief and prepares for the next onslaught of anxious, hurried researchers.

This whole process needs to be slowed down and approached more intelligently. Students need time to explore the information that they gather and to develop some ideas about their topic while they are using the library. Exploration incorporates the three R's of relaxing, reading, and reflecting.

Relaxing

Relaxing may seem an unusual attitude to recommend to students using libraries for researching topics but when students rush through a literature search, their thoughts about their topics have little opportunity to evolve and develop during the research process. As students slow down and relax, they can read and reflect on the information they are gathering. They can begin to define and extend their ideas about the topic while they are gathering information.

While assuming a relaxed attitude, students' must center attention on the task of exploring for a focus. They need a clear understanding of what they are looking for. A thoughtful, attentive, interested approach to the literature search, rather than a mindless, indiscriminate accumulation of sources, should be promoted. One student referred to a literature search as "ransacking the library." Unfortunately, ransacking describes many students' approach to locating materials. The ransacking approach can result in permanent damage to library materials and is not nearly as productive for students as a relaxed, thoughtful willingness to learn.

Another student described a more relaxed approach in which he was open to learning about the topic in the early stages of the research process in this way: "Every Sunday I started going to the library. Every time I went I'd sit by the literary stuff and pull things out on drama and look through them and see what they had to say about plays and drama. Most of the time they weren't helpful specifically but they gave me ideas. I usually sit by myself and read but I don't do serious reading until toward the end."

Reading

Reading to become informed about a topic is the primary strategy for exploring library materials to find a focus. Through reading, students learn about their topic; they define and extend their understanding. Their reading leads them to note interesting facts about the topic. They become aware of such things as influential people involved in the subject, particular related events, and any controversy surrounding the topic. They discover opposing points of view. All of these lead students to a focus for their research. Reading is an essential activity in the exploration stage. Rarely can a focus be identified without careful reading.

A common practice of students is to read after the literature search has been completed. Much of the difficulty students experience in writing research papers stems from this practice. They delay reading, thinking, and focusing their topics until they are ready to write. Without clear ideas of how they will focus the information they have gathered, they find that their thoughts are not sufficiently developed to write about the topic. Muddled, incoherent papers are a result of vague, underdeveloped ideas. Reading to find a focus should take place during the research process. Findings are presented after the literature search is completed, when the student writes the paper.

Reflecting

As students reflect on their reading, their thoughts about their topics evolve. Thoughts on a topic are extended through reading what others have written and reflecting on it. Reflection requires both preparatory reading and time. The term "reflection" evokes images of calm, quiet consideration. As one student put it, "I just let it sit for a while." Some students do not realize they are thinking about their topic at this time. There is a fine line, however, between reflecting and procrastinating. It is difficult even for experienced researchers to know when they are germinating an idea and when they are avoiding work on a difficult project. Many students describe having "aha" experience of ideas coming together suddenly when they least expect it.

The important concept here is that ideas about the topic need some time to develop. Reading and reflecting are companion activities that enable ideas to grow. As students become aware of their need to reflect, they will learn to allow time for this. They will also read during the process to promote their thinking.

Restructuring Library Use

The three R's of exploration are not likely to take place unless there is some restructuring of the time provided for students to use the media center in a research assignment. The class time spent in the media center is similar to a laboratory session in science. The media center is a laboratory for learning how to do library research.

In a typical research assignment, students are brought to the media center to locate materials on their chosen topics for one or more class periods. It is generally expected that they will return to the media center or other library on their own to continue their research. Having one formal library search session, however, creates the false impression that there is one type of search in which all materials may be gathered, after which reading, organizing, and writing take place.

Students must understand that they have different information needs at the various stages of the research process and the materials in a library can inform them at each stage. During a research assignment, three separate media center sessions might be scheduled to enable students to clearly differentiate between a preliminary search, an exploratory search, and a collection search. In each separate session the purpose and procedure of the particular search they are conducting can be explained, demonstrated, and experienced.

The exploratory library search should be separated from the collection search when teaching students to do library research. Skilled library researchers go to the library to read about a topic and reflect over a period of time. After some ideas have formed, they return to the library to gather information specifically related to their developing ideas and how they will present the topic. Similarly, students can come to the media center to explore topics and again a week or two later to collect information. If two or three separate search sessions are provided, students are able to learn the difference between the types of literature searches and the different purposes for which library materials may be used.

In the media center session for an exploratory search, students can learn techniques for locating information to expand their understanding and stimulate thinking. They can be urged to read what they find and to think about the new information and fresh ideas they encounter. They can be offered opportunities to write and talk about the ideas that are emerging.

Defining Possible Ways to Focus a Research Topic

After students have read and reflected on their topics, possible ways to focus their research should begin to occur to them. Through practice and experience, they learn to recognize a possible focus within the information they find on their topics. Identifying a research focus is difficult for new researchers. One student described his experience in this way: "Usually I don't have trouble with research assignments. But this time it's so focused that it is a lot harder. The research papers that I had to do were general. The teacher wants a narrow focus, in-depth, this time. It was tough to choose—not to choose—but to narrow down."

After doing some initial reading, students often find it helpful to talk about their topics. Many students discuss their topics with friends and parents on their own. Class discussion sessions may be arranged to give students an opportunity to talk about their ideas with their classmates. In preparation for the discussion sessions, students need to read and think about their topics. Expressing and explaining their ideas about a topic to another person serves to clarify their thoughts.

Discussion groups should be kept small, no larger than five students, to assure that each student has ample opportunity for participating in the talking. The comments of classmates often provide the feedback needed to determine the aspects of the topic that are of special interest and also the problems that might be encountered in further research. The discussion groups also serve the purpose of sharing a body of information with members of a class. Most research assignments are made to cover a particular area of the subject not contained in the text, which has significant bearing on the content of the course. Sharing the information that has been explored can be enriching for other students in the class. As students express their ideas and listen to their classmates' reactions, possible ways to focus their topic may become clearer to them.

After students define several possible ways in which their research topic might be focused, they need to explore in the library collection each possibility that they are considering. They will need information to predict the outcome of choosing each possible focus. Their choice will be based on their predictions. The accuracy of their predictions on how the research will result will depend on how effectively they have used library sources.

The library media specialist needs to be actively involved in students' exploratory library search. As the search progresses, students should seek more specific sources of information. Learning to progress from general sources to specific sources is a technique that the library media specialist can help students to learn.

Noting Ideas

Although students need not take extensive, detailed notes in the exploration stage, they should be urged to keep a record of their ideas. Their journals are an excellent place for recording reflections on their reading. After they read some material about their topic, they can log what they recall that is of particular interest and also note some of their personal reactions.

Writing is an excellent tool for clarifying thinking. Just as talking about a topic helps students to develop thoughts through their need to express them to others, writing helps students clarify their ideas through their need to record their thinking. You may want to give students some specific directions for writing about their topics. Several writing exercises for defining a focus are included in the activity section of this chapter.

Documenting Sources

From the beginning of the research process, students must keep a complete record of the library sources they use. In the exploration stage they should be advised to note the bibliographic citations of all of the materials they use to explore their topics. They will return to these sources at a later stage in the research process. Students need not retrace the location steps of using the catalog or other index each time they need to refer to a source. A source log (See Activity 3-7) is provided for listing materials as they are consulted. The source log also includes a space for briefly describing the content, which will help the student to recall the source at a later time when it is needed.

A style manual should be recommended and the form of bibliographic citation should be followed closely when students record sources in their source logs. (A list of style manuals is given at the end of Section 3.)

Students should be warned against plagiarizing an author's work. It is easy, unwittingly, to plagiarize an author's ideas. As students read and reflect, they take on the new ideas they meet as their own. They need to be cautioned against adopting ideas without identifying the source of their origin. The source log is a necessary companion to the journal. In the journal, students record ideas as they develop, intermingling personal reactions with the facts and ideas presented by the author. On the form, the students log the citations of the sources they use. Most students find the form especially useful for keeping track of all of the sources that they use during their library search.

Role of the Teacher and the Library Media Specialist

In the exploration stage of the library research process, the teacher and the library media specialist work as a team to help students prepare to form a focus for their research. The teacher structures the research activities to encourage students to relax, read, and reflect as they explore library materials. When students are guided to note ideas rather than detailed facts, they are led to define ways to focus their topics.

The library media specialist assists students in making an exploratory search of the library collection. By guiding students to identify descriptors and to consider the variety of sources in the library, you lead them to explore information on their topic for a focus.

The following activities assist students in exploring information on their topic in search of a focus.

ACTIVITY 3-1
TIME LINE OF THE RESEARCH PROCESS

The time line helps students to visualize the total research process. It enables them to see where they are in the process, to define the task before them, and to know what feelings to expect. The activity also helps students to gain a realistic sense of timing throughout the research process.

Time: 20 minutes

Materials: chalkboard

Note: This is an extension of Activity 1-5.

Conducted by: teacher or library media specialist

Activity Directions: Draw the time line of the research process on the chalkboard labeling the first, second, and third stages as shown here.

```
receive          select          explore for
assignment       topic           possible focus
   |               |               |
___|_____|_____|_____
```

Review the first two stages and briefly identify the third stage, saying something along these lines: "You have received your assignment, have selected a topic, and are now ready to explore the topic in search of a focus for your research." Point to the place on the time line that depicts the third stage.

Describe the task of the third stage. Here's one example of how you might begin: "Your task at this point is to read about your topic. Learn more about it and look for aspects of the topic that you find especially interesting. Notice author's ideas that are particularly thought-provoking. Think about some possible ways you might focus your research. You will need to explore the topic to identify and form a focus."

Describe the feelings that students are likely to experience in the third stage, perhaps saying "For many students this is the most difficult stage in the research process. When you first start to locate library materials on your topic, you are confronted with many different kinds of information. It can be quite confusing. Your ideas about your topic may be quite different from what you find in the books and other materials in the library. There is often so much information that you don't know where to begin. You will probably feel confused and uncertain and maybe even somewhat discouraged. Try to tolerate these feelings and begin reading to learn more about your topic."

Follow-up: This activity is intended to be followed up by activities to help students explore library materials for a research focus.

ACTIVITY 3-2
IDENTIFYING DESCRIPTORS

This activity helps students find subject headings to be used to search a library collection. Students learn to use general encyclopedias as a source of descriptors.

Time: 30–40 minutes or one class period

Conducted by: library media specialist with teacher

Materials: General encyclopedias in the media center reference collection (in hardcopy or CD-ROM format)

Activity Directions: Explain that information in a library collection is arranged by subject, time period, geographical location, and biographies of people involved. Tell your students: "An encyclopedia is an excellent source of this information. As you read an encyclopedia article about your topic, notice what, when, where, and who."

Explain to students that they will need to use subject headings to search the library collection. Tell them: "Subject headings are often called descriptors because they describe an aspect of a topic. Descriptors lead to information in indexes such as the computer or card catalog and periodical indexes."

"Try to identify five to ten different descriptors on your topic." (See the "Identifying Descriptors" Worksheet.) "Note the following in the encyclopedia article on your topic:

1. Terms and key words

2. Dates of important events

3. Location and specific names of places

4. Names of people who have made a contribution or been involved in some way

5. General subject or discipline in which your topic belongs. "Make a list of the descriptors that you find."

Follow-up: Collect the list of descriptors. Note omissions or mistakes that might be misleading. Return the lists to the students to be used as subject headings.

© 1994 by Carol Collier Kuhlthau

Name _____

Date _____

Topic _____

IDENTIFYING DESCRIPTORS

Descriptors are terms that describe your topic in some way. They are used as subject headings to find information in the catalog and other indexes. Look up your topic in a general encyclopedia. Identify five to ten different descriptors of your topic in the following categories:

1. Terms and key words

2. Dates of important events

3. Location and specific names of places related to your topic

4. Names of people who have made a contribution or been involved in some way

5. Subject or discipline of which your topic is a part

ACTIVITY 3-3
DEFINING A TOPIC

This activity directs students to use dictionaries to gain a clear definition of their topics. Students learn to seek an authoritative definition at the beginning of library research.

Time: 30–40 minutes or one class period

Note: This activity can be combined in one class period with Activity 3-2 "Identifying Descriptors."

Conducted by: library media specialist or teacher

Materials: unabridged dictionaries in the media center collection

Activity Directions: Explain to students that it is important to have an authoritative definition of their topics at the beginning of their library research. You might explain it this way: "An authoritative definition is one that has been accepted by a committee of distinguished scholars." Show the students the list of editors and compilers in an unabridged dictionary.

Explain that an unabridged dictionary provides fuller description and more information about the topic than an abridged dictionary.

Direct students to note the following:

1. Differences from your personal definition
2. Additional definitions that are new to you
3. Synonyms
4. Quotations using the term
5. Anything that is not clear to you

Encourage the students to confer with you on anything in the definition that is not clear to them.

Follow-up: Encourage the students to continue to use an unabridged dictionary to define other familiar terms they note in the encyclopedia article on their topic.

DEFINING YOUR TOPIC

1. Find a definition of your topic in an unabridged dictionary. Write the definition here.

2. Is the definition different from your understanding of the topic? List what is new to you.

3. What is not clear to you in the definition? List any terms or ideas that you do not clearly understand.

4. Locate and write the definition of these terms that are not clear to you.

Worksheet/Activity 3–3

© 1994 by Carol Collier Kuhlthau

ACTIVITY 3-4
EXPLORATORY LIBRARY SEARCH

This activity guides students through an exploratory search. They learn to approach the library as a whole information source. They are encouraged to read and reflect as they locate information on their topic in search of a focus.

Time: a minimum of one class period with additional time for reading

Conducted by: library media specialist with the teacher

Materials: media center collection

Activity Directions: Explain the purpose of an exploratory search. Here is a suggested explanation: "Now that you have chosen your research topic, you will need to learn more about it in order to find some area or focus to concentrate on. In an exploratory library search you seek materials to read that will increase your understanding of your general topic. Through your reading you will need to find a focus for your research."

Suggest that students think of a library as a whole information source. Say something like this: "Instead of dashing to the computer or card catalog to grab a couple of books about your topic, think of all of the different types of information there are in a library collection, such as reference, both general and subject, nonfiction, fiction, biography, magazines, newspapers, pamphlets, and audio-visuals. Ask yourself the following question at the beginning of your library search: 'How can each type of source inform me about my topic?' "

Recommend that students use their list of descriptors as subject headings: "Using your list of descriptors as subject headings, begin to search the various indexes to the media center collection, such as the catalog, periodical indexes, and indexes in reference books as well as in books in the general collection," Encourage the students to find several different types of sources on their topic. (See the "Exploring the Library" worksheet.) Offer assistance to students who experience difficulty.

Follow-up: Activity 3-5, "The Three R's of Exploration: Relax, Read, Reflect," is intended to follow this activity and may be used at the end of this class session rather than as a separate activity.

Name _____

Date _____

Topic _____

EXPLORING THE LIBRARY

Exploring information in the library will help you to form a focus for your research. You will need to read and to think about your topic to develop your ideas. The library has many kinds of information. How can each type of source inform you about your topic?

Using your list of descriptors as subject headings, locate information on your topic in the following indexes:

1. List some titles you find on your specific topic in the computer or card catalog. Use the back of this worksheet if necessary.

   CALL NUMBER   TITLE

2. Using a general subject heading, find titles in the computer or card catalog that might contain your topic. Locate the books and, using the index within the books, find pages that have information on your topic. List titles that contain information on your topic. Use the back of this worksheet if necessary.

   CALL NUMBER   TITLE   PAGES

3. List any reference sources that you find in the catalog relating to your topic. Using the index in these subject reference sources, locate the pages that have information on your topic. Use the back of this worksheet if necessary.

   CALL NUMBER   TITLE   PAGES

4. List magazine articles about your topic cited in the periodical index.

   ARTICLE TITLE   PAGE   MAGAZINE   DATE

Worksheet/Activity 3–4

© 1994 by Carol Collier Kuhlthau

ACTIVITY 3-5
THE THREE R'S OF EXPLORATION:
RELAX, READ, REFLECT

This activity is intended to follow the exploratory library search. Students are encouraged to relax, read, and reflect on the materials they have located.

Time: one class period with additional time for reading and reflecting

Conducted by: library media specialist with the teacher

Materials: media center collection and other materials students have gathered

Activity Directions: Explain to students that they need time to explore the information in the materials they gather to develop some ideas about their topic. Describe the three R's of exploration in this way or however you feel comfortable: "*Relax.* Don't rush through your search. Slow down and approach it intelligently. Think about the kind of information you are seeking and what sources are likely to be most useful. *Read.* Becoming better informed about your topic is your primary objective at this stage, so that you can choose a focus for your research. Read the materials that you find to learn more about your topic. *Reflect.* As you reflect on your reading, your thoughts about the topic will evolve and grow. Some ways to focus your topic will begin to occur to you."

The following questions help students to reflect on their reading:

1. What new interesting facts have I learned?
2. What people have been involved with the topic?
3. What events are related to the topic?
4. Are there any controversies surrounding the topic?
5. Do the authors present any opposing points of view?

Follow-up: Students must read to develop thoughts in preparation for forming a focus for their research. You may need to monitor students' reading to assure that they do not neglect this step. They may use their journals to write about their reading.

ACTIVITY 3-6
KEEPING A JOURNAL

This activity provides students with a tool for writing about the ideas as they encounter them in their reading. Students are encouraged to keep a record of interesting ideas rather than directly copying what they read. Writing about ideas is useful for leading students to form a focus for their research. Detailed notetaking is delayed until after a focus has been chosen.

Time: 30–40 minutes in class

Note: This activity can be combined in the same class period with the introduction to the source log

Materials: spiral notebook for each student

Preparation: A duplication of the following directions may be prepared and distributed (See the following worksheet.) or you may read the questions for the students to copy in their journals.

Activity Directions: Tell students: "You do not need to take extensive detailed notes while you are exploring your topic for a focus. You will need to keep a record of interesting ideas. These may be recorded in your journals. Write about each source you use. The following questions will help you to think and write about your reading.

1. What new facts have I learned?
2. What people have been involved with the topic?
3. What events are related to the topic?
4. Are there any controversies surrounding the topic?
5. Do the authors present any opposing points of view?"

Follow-up: Students should be encouraged to continue to write about each source they use.

© 1994 by Carol Collier Kuhlthau

Name _____

Date _____

QUESTIONS TO THINK ABOUT IN YOUR READING

Look over the list of library materials that you have found through the indexes in the library. Select one or two from each type of source to read and think about. As you read each source, write your answers to the following questions in your journal.

1. What new facts have I learned?

2. What people have been involved with the topic?

3. What events are related to the topic?

4. Are there any controversies surrounding the topic?

5. Do the authors present any opposing points of view?

ACTIVITY 3-7
SOURCE LOG

In this activity students are introduced to a log in which to record the bibliographic citations of their sources. They learn to keep a precise record of their sources from the beginning of their library research. They are cautioned against using an author's ideas as their own.

Time: 20 minutes to one class period

Conducted by: the teacher or library media specialist

Materials: four source logs and list of style manuals (Worksheets 1, 2, 3, & 4)

Preparation: Duplicate five copies of each source log for each student

Activity Directions: Caution students against plagiarizing an author's work, telling them: "As you begin your library research you will come across various kinds of material on your topic by many different authors. At the exploring stage, it is easy to take the new ideas that you encounter as your own. You will need to keep a record of every source you consult."

Distribute the source logs telling students "On the log you record the citation for each source as you use it. In most cases you will find the information to complete the citation on the title page of the source." Go over each column on the log explaining the information to be included. Give examples for each column.

Explain to students: "There is also a column to describe the information within the source. This is to help you recall the source when you need to return to it at a later point in your research process. Describe each source in a distinctive way that will be meaningful to you."

Variation: Some students may need a more in-depth explanation of plagiarism. Elaborate on this lesson according to students' needs.

Recommended Style Manuals

Campbell, William Giles, and Stephen Vaughan Ballou. *Form and Style: Theses, Reports, Term Papers.* Boston: Houghton Mifflin Co., 1990.

MLA Handbook for Writers of Research Papers, Theses, and Dissertations. Modern Language Association of America, 1988.

Publication Manual of the American Psychological Association. 2nd Edition. American Psychological Association, 1983.

Follow-up: The source logs may be submitted to the teacher or library media specialist each week to be reviewed and returned. Many students need to be monitored in this way as they begin library research. This also offers an opportunity to suggest sources that students might have overlooked.

© 1994 by Carol Collier Kuhlthau

Name _____

Date _____

Topic _____

SOURCE LOG (BOOKS)

Call Number _____   Description

Author _____   _____

Title _____   _____

Place of Publication _____   _____

Publisher _____   _____

Copyright Date _____   _____

Call Number _____   Description

Author _____   _____

Title _____   _____

Place of Publication _____   _____

Publisher _____   _____

Copyright Date _____   _____

Call Number _____   Description

Author _____   _____

Title _____   _____

Place of Publication _____   _____

Publisher _____   _____

Copyright Date _____   _____

Name _____

Date _____

Topic _____

SOURCE LOG (REFERENCE)

Call Number _____   Description

Author/Editor _____   _____

Title of Reference Source _____   _____

_____   _____

Title of Article _____   _____

Place of Publication _____   _____

Publisher _____   _____

Edition and Date _____   _____

Volume _____   _____

Pages _____   _____

Call Number _____   Description

Author/Editor _____   _____

Title of Reference Source _____   _____

_____   _____

Title of Article _____   _____

Place of Publication _____   _____

Publisher _____   _____

Edition and Date _____   _____

Volume _____   _____

Pages _____   _____

© 1994 by Carol Collier Kuhlthau

SOURCE LOG (PERIODICALS)

© 1994 by Carol Collier Kuhlthau

Author _____

Title of Periodical _____

Title of Article _____

_____

Date of Publication _____

Volume _____

Pages _____

Description

_____

_____

_____

_____

_____

_____

Author _____

Title of Periodical _____

Title of Article _____

_____

Date of Publication _____

Volume _____

Pages _____

Description

_____

_____

_____

_____

_____

_____

Author _____

Title of Periodical _____

Title of Article _____

_____

Date of Publication _____

Volume _____

Pages _____

Description

_____

_____

_____

_____

_____

_____

Name _____

Date _____

Topic _____

SOURCE LOG (AUDIO-VISUAL MATERIALS)

Title _____   Description

Format _____   _____

Place of Distribution _____   _____

Distributor _____   _____

Date _____   _____

Title _____   Description

Format _____   _____

Place of Distribution _____   _____

Distributor _____   _____

Date _____   _____

Title _____   Description

Format _____   _____

Place of Distribution _____   _____

Distributor _____   _____

Date _____   _____

© 1994 by Carol Collier Kuhlthau

STAGES OF THE
LIBRARY RESEARCH PROCESS:

Section 4
Forming a Focus

TASK	To formulate a focus from the information encountered.
THOUGHTS	Predict outcome of possible focuses • Use criteria of personal interest, requirements of assignment, availability of materials, and time allotted • Identify ideas in information from which to form a focus • Sometimes characterized by a sudden moment of insight.
FEELINGS	Optimism • Confidence in ability to complete task.
ACTIONS	Read lists for themes.
STRATEGIES	Make a survey of lists • List possible focuses • Choose a particular focus and discard others or combine several themes to form one focus.

SECTION 4

Forming a Focus

TASK OF THE FOURTH STAGE

In the fourth stage of the research process a focus for research needs to be found within the general topic. Students may decide to concentrate on some aspect of the topic, a particular perspective, or a theme to research and present.

Forming a focus for research marks a turning point in the research process. Before students form a focus, they gather general information on their topics. After they decide on a focus they gather specific information about their focus.

A focus is formed by exploring several possible choices and deciding on the one that appears to promise the most success. The decision to research a particular focus should be based on the findings of an exploratory search as described in Chapter 3. As students locate and read materials on the general topic, possible ways to focus the topic should become apparent. Additional information on each possible focus should be located and read. The exploratory search prepares students for predicting the outcome of choosing a particular focus. Deciding on a focus on the basis of an exploratory search should offer students the prospect of successful research and presentations.

Although a definite focus should be formed at this point in the research process, the focus need not remain static; it may continue to take shape as long as the research continues. By forming a focus, students identify an area of concentration in which their ideas can continue to grow and evolve. A focus will usually have to be altered in some way to match the information encountered in the collection stage of the library research; but if the focus has been carefully formed through an exploratory search, seeking a totally new focus should not be necessary.

Students need to have a clear understanding of their task in this stage. They need to be aware that a decision must be made before they proceed with their information collection. If they are not ready to decide on a focus, they should return to the third stage and continue to explore the general topic until they are able to form a focus for their research.

Feelings of Students While Forming a Focus

Forming a focus indicates a turning point in the feelings of students in the research process. As they decide on a focus for their research, they emerge from a sense of confusion and feeling of doubt into a sense of purpose and feeling of confidence. Students' feelings toward a research project change when they find a focus, as does their confidence in their ability to complete the task. Two students described their feelings in this way:

(Before a focus) "I was worried that I couldn't do a good job because I didn't know what I was doing." (After a focus) "I felt pretty happy about it. I began to find recurrent themes."

(Before the focus) "I was confused, lost, because I like to know that things are in order." (After the focus) "I was a lot more relieved because I had a goal. Once you know what you are looking for, it's so much easier to go about what you are doing."

Students tend to feel more relaxed after a focus has been formed. They have a sense of direction and a clearer understanding of their task. They are usually able to move on with their research more independently than before the focus was formed.

Making a Decision

There are two main decision points in the research process. The first is selecting a topic after the research assignment has been made. The second is forming a focus after information on the topic has been explored. Both decisions are made in a similar way. Students predict the outcome of their choices based on their constructs of the topic and their task. They choose the most appealing or appropriate outcome. They select the focus that appears to offer the most promising prospect, much as they did when choosing a topic.

Deciding on a focus has a significant impact on the research process. A focus closes down some possible directions as it opens up a particular area for concentrated examination. Once a focus has been formed, students must divert their attention from what has become extraneous within the general topic and turn their total attention to collecting only information pertinent to their focus.

Students should be cautioned against deciding on a focus without adequate preparation. The exploratory library search provides the basis for making the decision on a focus. Reading the information gathered in the library and reflecting on the ideas and facts presented enable students to increase their understanding of the general topic.

Intentionally seeking a focus is crucial in preparation for forming a focus. As students read about the general topic, they must look for a focus for their research. By using this approach, they will discover potential ways to focus their research.

To make a decision, students must have alternatives from which to choose. During the exploration stage, they build up their alternatives in order to make an intelligent choice of a focus. Thinking is very much involved at this point. Unless students have given their topic careful consideration and taken steps to enable their thoughts to develop, they will have difficulty forming a focus. The exploratory search provides information that allows students to define and extend each alternative focus in preparation for their decision.

Criteria for Forming a Focus

The criteria for forming a focus are the same four areas of consideration as those in selecting a topic. They are personal interest, requirements of the assignment, time allotted, and information available. The four questions for topic selection can be applied to forming a focus.

- Is the focus interesting?
- Does the focus meet the requirements of the assignment set down by the teacher?
- Can information be gathered and organized for presentation in the time allotted?
- Is there sufficient information on the focus in the media center or in other materials available?

Personal Interest

As students read about their topics, certain aspects and ideas will be more interesting to them than others. These areas of particular interest have potential for focusing their research. They should list interesting facts and ideas in their journals as they read about them. In addition, information of particular interest may be briefly noted in the column on the source log provided for describing the source.

Students will find it more useful to note what is of particular interest to them in an exploratory search than to attempt to take detailed notes on the information on their general topics. The personalized notes, often in the form of lists, lead students toward forming a focus.

By listing ideas and facts with the biographical citation of their sources, students are less likely to plagiarize an author's work. Ideas are recorded rather than copied. This method of notetaking is both more manageable and more useful in preparation for forming a focus.

Requirements of the Assignment

Students must keep in mind what the teacher has required that they accomplish in the research assignment. They need to continually measure the requirements of the assignment against what is personally interesting to them. Their focus must fit both criteria.

When students are considering a particular focus they should have an opportunity to confer with their teacher. At this time the teacher can direct them to accommodate the focus in any way that may be necessary to meet the requirements of the assignment.

Time Allotted

The amount of time students have to complete a research assignment affects their choice of a focus. They must learn to estimate the time they will need to research their focus and write their paper. The focus they choose must be researched within the time frame they have.

The time line of the research process helps students to develop a realistic sense of timing. (See Activity 4-1.) It enables them to visualize the task ahead and to pace themselves to accomplish their task.

Information Available to Support the Focus

The library search should be conducted to reveal whether a focus can be adequately researched in the media center or other libraries available to the students. A preliminary search to survey the amount of material available needs to be made on each focus under consideration. In this way students can know what information is available before they choose a focus.

When students form a focus without conducting a preliminary library search, they often have difficulty finding information to support their focus. A student explained his success at being able to support his focus in this way: "After I develop a focus, I usually find there is not enough information available. This time I surveyed what was available first." Students need to learn to survey what is available in the media center before they decide on a focus for their research.

An individual conference with the library media specialist is helpful at this point. As the students describe their library search, the library media specialist is aware of essential sources that may have been overlooked. At this stage, students usually are able to express the specific area of the topic that they are investigating. Their request, however, will not always match the way the library collection is organized. Frequently, the library media specialist can offer suggestions of subject headings and sources that bring the students in touch with the information they need.

An Aspect or a Theme?

Students need to have a clearer understanding of what a focus is and what it is they are seeking in the information they explore. They can picture a focus as forming in one of two ways. One way to visualize a focus is that of many paths merging into one. The other is that of selecting one path from many.

When students visualize a focus as many paths merging into one, they seek a unifying theme or thread for their research. They expect to form a focus that will reconcile the inconsistencies they encounter in the information they are gathering. They frequently describe their focus as serving to tie their research together. As one student expressed it, "It looked like you could tie all of the author's work by that theme." Some students described seeking a focus that would make their research come together. One student expressed apprehension at not finding a focus that would enable the research to come together. "It really didn't come together and I was getting nervous. I really didn't know how it was going to come together."

Another way to visualize a focus is that of choosing one path from many. In such cases, students seek one aspect of a topic to concentrate on as their focus.

To some extent, the research topic may determine the way a focus is formed. For some topics, such as those in literary research, it may be more appropriate to seek a recurring theme to tie the topic together. For other topics, such as those in historical research, a particular aspect or point of view of the topic might be more fitting. However, in most research assignments, a combination of a theme and a particular point of view must be sought in forming a focus.

Saving Time and Effort

When students understand the economy in forming a focus after exploring information and before collecting information, they are more than willing to make the extra effort to identify a manageable focus at this stage. They need to have a very clear understanding of why a focus is needed for their research. Through experience and guidance, they learn that a focus will ultimately save them from spending unnecessary time and effort. When they choose a focus during the research process, their information collection becomes more purposeful and efficient. Only information that directly relates to their focus is collected. Students are able to exclude irrelevant material and to select only that information which is pertinent to their focus.

Postponing a Focus

Many students postpone forming a focus until they have collected all of their information and begin to write their papers. They frequently describe these papers as impossible to write. At the time of writing, they may have gathered a pile of books and other materials and taken some random notes from a variety of sources. But they haven't read consistently or given their topic much thought. Now they must read, interpret, and present the diverse information they have collected. Many of these students never find a focus for their writing. They take a little from each source, often plagiarizing in their attempt to get something down. Their writing commonly lacks a central theme or an area of concentration. As a result, all too frequently, little significant understanding or interpretation of information is apparent in the research papers of many secondary students.

Forming a focus during the research process enables students to think through their research long before they sit down to write. When they have completed their library research process, they have a clear idea of the way they will focus their topic in their papers. Their ideas have evolved through the information they have gathered. When they are ready to write, their thoughts are well developed and clearly focused. Writing blocks are often a result of thinking blocks. When a topic is clearly thought through and the research has been focused on the developing thoughts, writing flows more smoothly and coherently.

Forming a Focus

The terms *selecting, choosing,* and *deciding* have been used to describe the task of focusing research. These terms were also used to describe the action taken in identifying a topic. *Forming,* however, implies something more. It is a creative process that involves extensive thinking.

Through the exploratory stage, students develop thoughts about their topics that are personally interesting. They pull ideas and facts from their reading that are interpreted through their own constructs. They begin to develop a personal view of the topic. From this view, students form a focus to research and present. Forming a focus often involves highly individualized thinking.

In research assignments in which a group of students have the same general topic, each may develop a personal perspective on the topic during the exploratory search. The research focus formed by each student is likely to be quite different from that of the others. Although they started with the same topic, their research papers may differ widely.

Forming is the creative activity of thinking of a focus for research based on what students already know about a topic and what they want to learn about a topic. It requires attention, interest, and concentration. Forming is a highly individualized process that students must do for themselves. A teacher and library media specialist can lead students in their thinking about a focus, but the students must form the focus by combining their existing thoughts with what they are reading.

To form a focus, students must be willing to close down some possibilities for research. They need to give up certain aspects of the topic or to set some things aside for another time. As one focus is singled out for concentration, all other possible areas must be disregarded.

Needing to Return to a Prior Stage

If students cannot form a focus at this point, they will need to return to a prior stage. Further exploration into the topic may develop their thoughts, enabling them to form a focus. If, after further reading and thinking, they are still unable to form a focus, they may need to consider selecting an entirely different topic. Sometimes students reach a dead end in their research and need to make a fresh start rather than belaboring a topic that has gone stale for them.

One such student described the need to abandon his initial topic and begin the research process again. He had chosen the Elizabethan period for his topic and was moving toward focusing on the theater, possibly the influence of the privy council, when he decided to abandon the topic. He expressed his feelings in this way: "So I went to look for a total change because I was really sick of it, the whole Elizabethan period. I had trouble with it. I was sick of it. I didn't want to do it anymore."

When students become discouraged and their topics have lost all appeal, it is sometimes best for them to choose a new topic. In the case of the student cited above, a perfectly legitimate topic was abandoned. To experience some discouragement and tedium is natural in the research process and must be tolerated and worked through. There is a fine line between a topic that no longer interests a student and one that merely needs some expert direction. The library media specialist or the teacher can salvage many topics by offering suggestions to put a discouraged student on the right track. To insist, however, that students hold to topics that have become tedious for them serves no positive purpose. Students must understand that choosing a new topic means starting the research process over again and repeating the initial stages.

The Turning Point of the Research Process

Forming a focus marks a transition in the research process. As previously described, the feelings of students change at this point. Prior to the focus, they often feel confused and uncertain. After the focus, they usually feel more clear and confident. This is a transition stage for the thoughts and actions of students as well.

Focus formulation originates in the exploration stage and merges into the collection stage. As a focus is formed, the purpose of the library research turns from exploring to collecting, the materials used go from general to specific, and the information sought changes from relevant to pertinent.

To make students more aware of the turning point in their research, ask them to identify the point at which they formed a focus on the time line of the research process. They can be led to visualize the research up to this point and after this point, and in this way become more conscious of the transition that takes place.

The "Aha" Experience

Sometimes a focus is formed in a moment of insight or what has been called the "aha" experience of creative thinking. Some students described a moment of insight when they suddenly had a clear idea of how they would focus their research in this way: "I didn't know what I was going to do. I wanted to do a good paper and have a good focus. It was kind of frustrating. And then it just hit me that this would be a good idea." Another student described a similar moment of clarity. ". . . and then it hit me. All of the information I was looking at was in contrast to what most people think. I decided to focus on that."

The moment of insight, or the "aha" experience, is built on a basis of knowledge of the topic. These students had been reading and thinking about their topics and were considering alternatives for focusing their research. The moment of insight came. They decided on their focus and had a clearer perception of what they were doing from that point. Actively seeking a focus through an exploratory search of library materials may result in a moment of insight that leads to a focus.

Students who form a focus during the research process can usually identify a point when they have a clearer perception of what they want to do. This point is often connected with a particular source in which an idea pulls the topic together or identifies a particularly interesting aspect for a research focus.

The following describes a student's experience: "I had an idea in my head but I didn't know how to phrase it. I was reading an article that reviewed *The Grapes of Wrath*. There was a paragraph that fit exactly. It was what I had in my head but I couldn't get it into words. I found it!"

Students need to understand that a focus should be based on thoughts formed through extensive exploratory reading. Choosing a focus without careful research will often result in centering research on something that cannot be supported, or perhaps even investigated, in library research. The "aha" experience usually occurs after students have become familiar with general information on the topic.

Adapting and Refining a Focus

The focus should not be thought of as a static, unchanging statement. After the focus has been formed it continues to be refined and extended throughout the balance of the research process.

After students identify a concentration for their research, they continue to encounter new ideas. As further information is sought to confirm the focus, contradictory information may also be found. The information may indicate that the focus needs to be adapted in some way. Students must decide how to handle contradictory information. They need to consider whether the focus should be refined or whether contrary information should be presented and the original focus defended. Both adapting and refining the focus takes place throughout the collection stage of the research process.

One problem with requiring students to make a formal thesis statement at the beginning of the research process is that there is no provision for adapting and refining the focus. When the thesis statement is considered adjustable, more like a research focus, it can be altered according to new information encountered in the library research. Having students identify what they are researching within a general topic is necessary for directing their thinking. When the thesis statement, however, is made without an exploratory search and adapting and refining are not allowed within the research process, students often have difficulty locating supporting evidence.

Students need to adapt and refine their focus through the information they collect. One student, who had identified a focus on which to center his collection of information, explained that his focus continued to change: "My real focus didn't become clear until a couple of days before I started writing the paper." By "real focus" he meant his refined focus, as presented in his research paper. While students need to concentrate on information that is pertinent to their focus, they must remain open to new ideas about the research focus they have chosen.

Process of Forming a Focus

The process of forming a focus has been described in this chapter as identifying some possibilities by exploring the general topic, predicting the outcome of each possible research focus, and choosing the one that is thought to hold the most promising prospect. One student described the steps she took in forming a focus for research (her general topic was the writings of Mark Twain): "I remember I sat in my room one day and said I might as well get started. I looked over the books and decided what my focus would be." She explained that at first she thought she would do a critical analysis: "But when I read over the books of criticisms, I realized that I didn't want to do that because I would have to compare *Huck Finn* with *Tom Sawyer* and I hadn't read *Tom Sawyer*." She described her feelings at the time: "I could not really understand what the separate articles in the book were about. I was frustrated because I had reached a dead end in my research. I realized that a criticism of the book would be impossible." Then she looked through a biography and stated, "This book about his life and his writing gave me ideas." Her journal entry states, "I looked in the index under Huck Finn and read the sections on it. It seems that many of the events in the book were real events in Sam Clemens' life. I also took a great interest in the Colonel Sherburn chapters of the book."

She then listed three possible themes in her journal.

1. Real people and events that became part of Huck Finn.
2. Analysis of one chapter and its characters completely. (Colonel Sherburn)
3. Twain's voice in the novel through the characters.

She made a journal entry that described her feelings when she discovered this. "OPTIMISM—I might be able to do this paper by Christmas."

Later, she talked to some friends about the project and began to see that the three ideas could be combined into one focus centering around the Colonel Sherburn character. She explained that at this point she became more interested in the research project. Her journal entries describing the development of the focus for her research were made on November 23 and relate to what took place on two days, November 22 and November 23. She summarizes forming a focus in this way: "I started researching and in one book, I found that the Colonel Sherburn chapters were based on a real-life incident. I also found in another book that Mark Twain used Colonel Sherburn to express his views. I thought 'this has everything.' So I decided to concentrate on the two chapters in *Huck Finn* that relate to the Colonel Sherburn incident."

Some of the strategies this student used can be recommended to other students to help them form a research focus. Writing and talking are useful techniques for organizing thoughts to make a decision.

Strategies to Form a Focus

Many students haven't developed strategies on their own and benefit from assistance and suggestions of ways to focus their research. They need to pause in their library research and to organize their thoughts in some way. One student explained how his father helped him organize his thoughts: "My dad helped me a lot. I showed him what I was doing and he would be able to guide me. Actually he's the one who would organize it. He'd take out a paper and he'd say, 'Okay, these are the ways you are headed. Now which one do you want?' He'd just kind of lay it out for me and ask me, 'Which way do you want to do it?' But he would try not to influence me." The strategy of listing possible choices can be taught to students who are ready to focus their research. (See Activity 4-2).

Reviewing what they have read helps students organize their thoughts. If they have kept a journal, rereading their entries is often a helpful review. They can also refer to the source log on which they have recorded the citations of the sources they have used. The entries in the description column should aid them in recalling ideas encountered in the exploratory search. Listing the ideas for a focus is a strategy used by many students. After the ideas have been organized through listing or some other means, students often discuss the possible focus with friends and parents. Talking helps them to collect and clarify their ideas in preparation for making their decision. Opportunities for discussion can be provided within the classroom or media center for students who are new to library research. The teacher and library media specialist can become involved in the focusing process during writing exercises and discussion sessions.

Role of the Teacher and the Library Media Specialist

When students confer with the teacher, they can be assured that their focus is within the boundary of the content objectives of the assignment. When they confer with a library media specialist, they can be assured that their focus is within the boundary of the information in the media center collection.

The teacher and library media specialist can help students learn how to focus a research topic by recommending strategies that have brought success to other researchers. Students can become proficient and independent in forming a focus for their research.

The following activities are designed to assist students in forming a focus.

ACTIVITY 4-1
TIME LINE OF THE RESEARCH PROCESS

The time line helps students visualize the total research process. It enables them to see where they are in the process, to define the task before them, and to know what feelings to expect. The activity also helps students to gain a realistic sense of timing throughout the research process.

Time: 20 minutes

Materials: chalkboard

Note: This is an extension of Activity 1-5.

Conducted by: teacher or library media specialist

Activity Directions: Draw the time line of the research process on the chalkboard, labeling the first four stages as shown here.

receive assignment	select topic	explore for possible focus	form focus

Review the first three stages and briefly introduce the fourth stage: "You have received your assignment, selected a topic, and explored information on the topic in search of a focus. You should now be ready to form a focus for your research." Point to the place on the time line that depicts the fourth stage.

Describe the task of the fourth stage: "Your task is to decide to concentrate on some aspect of the topic or to choose a particular perspective or theme to research and present. You will need to use what you have learned about your topic to form your research focus."

Describe the feelings that students are likely to experience in the fourth stage: "When you form a focus for your research, you will probably notice a change in your feelings. Many students find that their feelings shift from a sense of confusion to a sense of direction and purpose. You can expect to feel more confident in what you are doing. You may even find that you are becoming more interested in your research. When you form a focus, you are on your way to completing your task."

Follow-up: This activity is intended to be followed by activities to help students form a focus for their research.

ACTIVITY 4-2
LISTING EACH POSSIBLE FOCUS

This activity assists students in organizing their thoughts in preparation for choosing a focus. It helps them predict the outcome of each possible focus.

Time: one class period or a homework assignment

Materials: Students may use their journals or the worksheet for this activity.

Conducted by: teacher

Activity Directions: Say to the students, "Think of three to five possible ways to focus your topic. List each possible focus at the top of a separate sheet of paper. Consider the following questions for each possible focus. Write your answers under the listed focus."

1. What do I know about the focus?
2. What new ideas and facts have I learned about the focus?
3. What sources have information on the focus?
4. Where can I expect to find more information about the focus?

Variation: Students may be asked to develop a question about their topic and then change the question into a focusing statement.

Follow-up: Recommend that students compare each focus to decide which is the most promising prospect for research.

© 1994 by Carol Collier Kuhlthau

Name _____

Date _____

CONSIDERING A FOCUS

Focus _____

1. What do you know about the focus?

2. What new ideas and facts have you learned from your reading?

3. What sources have information on the focus?

4. Where can you expect to find more information about the focus?

ACTIVITY 4-3
FORMING A FOCUS

This activity helps students understand what is involved in forming a focus. They become aware of the difference between an aspect of a topic as a focus and a central theme as a focus. Students review the ideas they encountered in their exploratory search in preparation for forming a focus.

Time: one class period or a homework assignment

Materials: students' journals and source logs

Conducted by: teacher

Note: Most of the activities for focusing a topic are usually conducted by the teacher, but the library media specialist can conduct them if both agree.

Activity Directions: Describe the process of forming a focus: "The terms *selecting, choosing,* and *deciding* are used to describe the task of forming a focus, but *forming* implies something more. Forming involves combining your existing thoughts with what you are reading to develop a focus for your research."

Explain that a focus can be an aspect of the topic or a central theme within the topic. Describe the difference between an aspect and a theme: "Picture a focus as forming in one of two ways. One way is that many paths emerge into one. In this case, the focus is a central theme or a unifying thread in the information that you have been reading, something that ties the ideas together." Cite an example from the assignment that students are working on:

"The other way a focus is formed is by selecting one path from many. One aspect of the topic is chosen to concentrate on as a research focus." Cite an example from the assignment that students are working on.

Direct students to read the journal entries they have been keeping and review their source log in which they have been recording citations and descriptions of the sources they have used. Have them note any themes or aspects they find. (See Worksheet 4-3.)

Follow-up: If students cannot find ways to focus their research at this point, suggest that they return to the media center for further exploration of information. Remind them to continue to make entries in their journals and on their source logs.

ASPECTS AND THEMES

Review your journal entries and the bibliography form descriptive column. List aspects and themes that you find.

1. Aspects of the topic.

2. Central themes and perspectives on the topic.

© 1994 by Carol Collier Kuhlthau

ACTIVITY 4-4
SURVEY OF MATERIAL ON A FOCUS

In this activity students learn to apply survey techniques to determine the amount of information on a focus. Surveying a library collection enables them to predict more accurately the outcome of each research focus they are considering.

Time: one class period

Material: This activity takes place in the media center, using the computer or card catalog and the periodical index.

Conducted by: library media specialist with the teacher

Activity Directions: Explain that a survey of the media center collection will help students know how much information on their focus is in the media center. Here's a sample of what to say: "By checking the catalog and the periodical index you found what information was available on your topic. You will use a similar method to determine the amount of information on your focus. Remember that you will not need to read the materials or to take notes. This time, however, you will need to locate some of the books.

"First, use the catalog to see if there are any titles that relate directly to your focus. If there are more than five titles, your focus may be too general.

"Then find the call number or numbers of the books on your general topic that might contain information on your focus. Locate the books and use the indexes in the back of the books to determine the amount of material that is specifically related to your focus. Look for pages in sequence, such as 23–29. You should be able to find several references on a focus to consider it as your choice for a research focus.

"In the periodical index read the titles of the articles on your general topic and count the ones that seem to be directly related to your focus. Remember that the index is more useful for current topics and may not list information regarding a retrospective focus." Explain that a retrospective focus is based on past situations or events.

"From these sources you should gain a sense of what is available on your focus, although there are many other sources you will want to use when you are actually collecting information."

Questions: The following questions help students center on the task of surveying a library collection for a focus. (You might want to distribute copies of "Making a Survey of a Library Collection," Worksheet 4-4.)

1. How many titles in the catalog directly relate to the focus? List three.

2. How many indexes in books on the general topic contain some information on the focus? List three.

3. How many articles in the index directly relate to the focus? List three.

Name _____

Date _____

MAKING A SURVEY OF A LIBRARY COLLECTION

For each focus you are considering, make a survey of the library collection and answer the following questions.

1. How many titles in the catalog directly relate to the focus? _____ List three.

   Call number   Title

2. How many indexes in books on the general topic contain some information on the focus? _____ List three.

   Call number   Title

3. How many articles in the index to periodicals directly relate to the focus? _____ List three.

   Title   Periodical   Date   Pages

© 1994 by Carol Collier Kuhlthau

ACTIVITY 4-5
DISCUSSION GROUPS

Small group discussions give students an opportunity to talk about the possible ways to focus their topics. Talking helps students clarify their ideas and leads them toward making a decision about forming a focus for their research.

Time: one class period

Conducted by: teacher

Activity Directions: Have students divide into groups of four or five members each. Direct the groups to discuss the possible ways they might focus their topics. Explain that within the small groups they can share some of the things they have learned in their reading. They should also describe the information available in the library on each possible focus. They should explain why they are considering the focus and where they expect their research to lead them. (You might want to give each group a copy of "Discussion Groups," worksheet 4-5 to help the group conduct the discussion.)

Allow 15 to 20 minutes for group discussion. Urge members of the groups to offer suggestions and ask questions about each other's focus. Call the class together and have each group report briefly on the progress of their members in forming a focus.

Name _____

Date _____

DISCUSSION GROUPS

Discussion groups are made up of four or five students. Each student takes a turn to:

1. State your possible focus and explain why you are considering the focus.

2. Describe where you expect your research to lead if you choose the focus.

Each member of the group should have an opportunity to ask questions and to offer suggestions after each focus is discussed.

© 1994 by Carol Collier Kuhlthau

ACTIVITY 4-6
CONFERENCING

Before students make a final decision on a research focus, they should confer with the teacher to be certain that they are meeting the requirements of the assignment. This activity provides students with an opportunity to confer with the teacher.

Time: 10–15 minutes for each conference

Materials: copies of "Preparing for a Conference," Worksheet 4-6

Conducted by: teacher and library media specialist

Activity Directions: Schedule individual conferences with each student. Ask students to respond to the following questions:

1. What have you learned in your reading that has led to the focus you are considering?
2. What materials on your focus are in the library?
3. How will you proceed with your research and what do you expect to find?

Note any misleading interpretations that students might have made. Recommend any needed retracing of steps.

Follow-up: If students' answers are inadequate or inaccurate, they will need to return to the media center for further reading and surveying materials.

Name _____

Date _____

PREPARING FOR A CONFERENCE

Before the conference be able to answer the following questions:

1. What have you learned in your reading that has led to the focus you are considering?

2. What materials on your focus are in the library?

3. How will you proceed with your research and what do you expect to find?

© 1994 by Carol Collier Kuhlthau

ACTIVITY 4-7
DECIDING ON A FOCUS

In this activity students are required to state their focus and to write a paragraph describing the focus. They must make a definite decision on their research focus at this point.

Time: 20 minutes or a homework assignment

Conducted by: teacher

Activity Directions: Have students state their focus and write a descriptive paragraph about it. (You might want to use Worksheet 4-7.) Ask them to include what they know about the focus from their exploratory reading. Have them write about the further information they are seeking and what they expect to find.

Collect the papers. Check to determine that each focus is sufficiently clear to offer students direction, but open to adapting and refining. Make suggestions and recommendations as necessary and return the papers to the students.

Follow-up: Some students may need additional individual assistance from the teacher and the library media specialist to form a workable research focus.

© 1994 by Carol Collier Kuhlthau

Name _____

Date _____

Topic _____

DECIDING ON A FOCUS

State your focus.

Write a paragraph on what you know about the focus and what further information you are seeking.

STAGES OF THE LIBRARY RESEARCH PROCESS:

Section 5
Collecting Information

TASK	To gather information that defines, extends, and supports the focus.
THOUGHTS	Seek information to support focus • Define and extend focus • Gather pertinent information • Organize information in notes.
FEELINGS	Realization of extensive work to be done • Confidence in ability to complete task • Increased interest.
ACTIONS	Use library to collect pertinent information • Request specific sources from librarian • Take detailed notes with bibliographic citations.
STRATEGIES	Use descriptors to search out pertinent information • Make comprehensive search of various types of materials, i.e., reference, periodicals, nonfiction, biography • Use indexes • Request assistance of librarian.

SECTION 5

Collecting Information

TASK OF THE FIFTH STAGE

In the fifth stage of the research process, students gather information that relates to their focus. After the focus has been formed, they return to the library to search the collection for pertinent information. They read and take notes on facts and ideas about their focus, keeping bibliographic citations of the sources they use.

The information collection stage should be entered only after students have identified a clear research focus. During this stage, the type of information sought shifts from that which is relevant to the general topic, to that which is pertinent to the focus. As one student explained, "On December 9, I got my main focus. Before this I did basic research. After I got my focus, I got all of my sources to support the focus I had found." Students need to have a clear understanding of their focus in order to discriminate between general information on the topic and specific information related to the focus.

A good focus can be adapted and altered while students are collecting information. Although students must keep the focus clearly in mind, they also must be able to refine and revise it as they read and take notes. In most cases, the focus will change somewhat as they gather information in this stage. When students expect change to take place, they actively seek to refine and adapt their focus through the information they collect.

Throughout this stage, students continue to learn about their focus as they gather information. Thinking remains central to the research process. As they read, their thoughts are more clearly defined and extended by new information. They take notes on the ideas and facts that contribute to building up their thoughts about the focus.

The task of collecting information must be approached systematically. Students can learn methods of searching a library collection to gather information on their focus from a variety of sources. They need to approach the library collection as a whole and to ask how each type of source might inform them about their focus. They need to become proficient at identifying, reading, and taking notes on the specific information they want to use to present their focus in the research paper.

Feelings of Students as They Collect Information

The feelings that students commonly experience in this stage are an increased confidence in their ability to complete the task. They have a more realistic concept of the amount of work ahead of them. Forming a focus makes their task more manageable and gives them a sense of direction.

Students frequently feel more relaxed at this stage. The confusion they felt before forming a focus is behind them and they feel more comfortable in the task of researching in the library. One student described his feelings in this way: "I felt relieved. It makes things a lot easier once you have a basis for where you are going." Another student explained that, "After you know exactly what you are going to do it on, the research is easy."

Many students also experience a feeling of increased interest in their subject. As they learn more about it and their thoughts are confirmed or challenged, their interest is piqued. By the end of this stage, many students have developed strong personal views on the focus and are eager to share those views with others.

Having a Clear Focus

When students have thoughtfully formed a focus, they are ready to enter the information collection stage of the research process. A clear focus gives students a basis for determining what information is useful and what is not useful for understanding and presenting their focus. The focus directs and shapes the choices they make throughout the information collection process.

Without a focus, students are unable to make decisions about the usefulness of information. They often establish arbitrary criteria for the usefulness of material. A lack of focus caused one student to assess usefulness on a general premise of whether the source related good things or bad things about the author he was researching: "In *Book Review Digest,* you could tell if they were positive or negative. I wasn't looking for negative because I wanted positive reviews."

Students who have difficulty collecting information frequently do not have a clear focus in mind. They lack the structure upon which to build their ideas.

Making Choices

Collecting information from a library involves a series of choices. As students search library materials, they must choose what they will read. As they read, they must choose what they will take notes on and what they will use to present their focus. Their notes are an accumulation of the choices they make as they use library materials.

Students need to become keenly aware of the choices they are making in the collection stage. They must learn to consider each choice on the basis of their focus. They should avoid including extraneous, irrelevant material in their notes. On the other hand, they must be conscientious in taking accurate, complete notes on information that relates directly to their focus. One student described making choices: "I took what was important. I used my own judgment. Once I narrowed it down, I knew things that were irrelevant I was not going to fit in."

Making choices in collecting information relating to a focus requires the use of the skills of abstract thinking. These are among the most complex and sophisticated skills that students acquire. They need to have reached maturity in their thinking abilities, what Piaget describes as the formal operational stage of cognitive development. Most students do not reach this level of development until they are 12 years old and many are somewhat older.

Students need a clear idea of what they are abstracting from the library collection. They also benefit from experience in abstracting information. The skill is based on a combination of cognitive maturity and practice. To abstract only that which pertains to the focus requires alertness and concentration. Students need to give their full attention to the choices they make. Abstracting information is not a task to be approached casually or taken lightly.

Refining and Adapting the Focus

While the focus must be kept clearly in mind, it must also be adapted by the information encountered. A focus is not a rigid, unchanging statement. It will be refined and altered as students read, think, and learn. As they collect information on their focus, they are likely to come across material that sheds new light on the focus. One student explained how his focus changed while he was gathering information in this way: "In the third week, I went to the library and I came across something by Jerome Singer in footnotes and I looked it up in the card catalog. It was in the child psychology section. I read it and it was useful. It dealt with aggresive behavior of children in controlling fantasy. . . . So that's when I started basing my paper on the misconception in children's literature of fairy tales. My real focus didn't come clear until a couple of days before I started writing the paper." The "real" focus is the refined focus that has been adapted as the student continued to learn through his reading.

Students need to expect their thoughts about the focus to continue to be defined and extended as they collect information. They must understand that there is a difference between adapting a focus and abandoning a focus as they evaluate the information they gather in the library.

Students who do not expect their focus to change can become discouraged at not finding evidence to support it. As one student related, "The more I looked, the less I found. When I didn't find it, I was kind of upset."

Another student, who was ready to accommodate her focus to new information, said, "My focus was three different parts of the same thing. Many books had something on one of the parts if not the whole focus. It was kind of broad in a way."

There are times, however, when students form a focus that can't be refined or adapted. Insufficient information is available on the focus and it must be totally changed. This is commonly the result of inadequate exploration at an earlier stage. In such cases, the information that students collect often leads them to a new focus that can be researched and supported within the library collection. One student described finding a new focus in the information she was collecting: "I looked in other reference books, that had something on hero and code hero, but not much. I went to the card catalog for literary criticisms and found nothing about code hero in books on the shelf. I noticed that all of the sources had something on symbolism. A good focus might be how symbolism predicts what will happen to the characters. But upon reading the book more carefully, the book really tells you what happens to them so there's no need to use symbolism for that. I kept reading critical analyses. I found two critics who contradicted each other. Then I took a third critic who was between them and based my research paper on that." The student had formed the first focus only to find it unsupportable in the information available to her. Her library search led her to consider other possible ways to focus her topic.

Setting an Invitational Mood

Students must be open to what the information reveals about their focus. An invitational mood allows them to alter the focus by being willing to learn and actively think about what they read.

The invitational mood is essential in the beginning of the research process to enable students to identify a topic that holds some personal interest for them. The mood continues to be important for promoting thinking and personal involvement in this central stage in the research process. While students, on the one hand, are seeking to complete their research task, they also are ready to continue to learn by defining and extending their ideas. As students move toward completing their research, they remain open to what the information reveals about the focus. The invitational mood allows them to refine and adapt the focus as they encounter new information.

Increasing Interest

As students collect information on their focus, many find that their interest in their topic increases. Two students reported on their increased interest as they progressed through the research process "I sat down and read over carefully and became totally interested in what I was reading." Another student explained that, "I didn't find this boring. I have 'senioritis' and really didn't feel like doing it but it was interesting—what I found." Students become more interested in their topics as their thoughts are defined and extended by the information they locate in their library research.

Thinking of the Library as a Whole

When students begin to search the library to locate information on their focus, they need to learn to think of the whole library as an information source. The library is a collection of various kinds of information that may be located by a number of access tools, such as the use of various indexes.

Many students have an extremely narrow view of the scope of information available to them. They need to become aware of a wide range of materials and to form habits of searching that explore the many varieties of sources in the library collection and access points to other collections. Unfortunately, there are a surprising number of students who use the general subject headings in the card catalog as their exclusive access point to the library collection. Their limited understanding of information storage and organization needs to be broadened.

Encouraging students to think of the library collection as a whole can increase the number of access points they use. They need to learn that a complete library search extends beyond the general nonfiction collection to encompass reference sources, data bases, periodicals, vertical file materials, biography sources, audiovisual software, and occasionally fiction.

Students need to develop a healthy respect for the organized collection of information provided for them in libraries across the country and throughout the world. The respect of users is essential not only for optimum use but also for the future preservation of information retrieval systems.

Searching a Library Collection

A library search takes time, interest, and a bit of the detective's investigative instinct. Searching requires the patience to stay with a task to its conclusion. Students may follow many false leads before locating the information they are seeking. They must be willing to try alternatives rather than assuming that the library does not have anything on their topic.

Students need a realistic understanding of what constitutes a successful library search. Many new researchers judge their search to be a failure if they do not find a book with the exact title of their focus. They hold an ideal of information retrieval that can rarely be realized. Their understanding of information organization and retrieval in libraries needs to be expanded.

A systematic approach to searching a library collection is needed at this stage. Students need to use a number of descriptors. They must follow the new leads they come across and use alternative approaches. They need to exhaust the many different types of sources in the library collection.

Using Descriptors and Leads

Descriptors that were identified and listed in the exploration stage can be used as subject headings in the collection stage. These descriptors lead to information on the general topic that may contain information on the focus. Students will also need descriptors that will lead them to specific information on their focus. They should note additional descriptors found in their search of the library collection and in the information they collect.

Finding descriptors along the way leads students on an intricate path through the library materials. One student described how he followed leads to locate information on his focus: "I looked up Mark Twain in the card catalog and took down every number. I took all of the books to a table and I looked in the indexes. The first book I looked in had a whole section on the shooting in Hannibal that he used for *Huck Finn*. . . . When I first found out about the incident, I wasn't sure what to look under. I couldn't find anything under Colonel Sherburn. But I noticed that the name Smarr was listed under Sherburn. I knew that was the man who was shot and that's what it was listed under. I was lucky."

Students also use bibliographies and footnotes to give them titles of sources that might be useful. One student said: "One book had a bibliography of the books that helped the author write that book. I looked up those books but they weren't there. I knew that if those books helped the author to write the book they would help me write my paper." Students frequently reported having difficulty locating sources from bibliographies and footnotes. They can be encouraged to seek the assistance of librarians who may be able to borrow the books through interlibrary loan. Students can become aware of the network of which the library they are using is a part.

Understanding the Organization of Information

To approach a library search intelligently, students need to have a general understanding of how information is organized. Too often, secondary students do not understand the basics of how a library works even though they have had prior, often extensive, library skills instruction. Their experience has been isolated to individual sources and limited to one system. Few students have acquired an overview of the universal patterns of the organization of information in libraries.

While there is no need for students to memorize the Dewey Decimal System, there is a need for them to become aware that an acquaintance with one classification system easily transfers to other systems, such as Library of Congress or computer classification systems. The basic concept that information in libraries is organized by numerical coding and alphabetical arrangement is extremely important for students to learn. To make a comprehensive search of a library collection, students must also understand that indexing provides access by subject, title, and author.

In addition, an understanding of the hierarchy of subject headings is necessary to learn that broad general subject headings, such as zoology, are broken down into subheadings, such as mammals, and further narrowed to specific categories, such as tigers. They must learn to move up and down the subject heading hierarchies in search of information. At times, a broader subject heading will be needed to locate material. At other times, a more precise term will lead to the needed information. Alternatives may be tried until all possible access points have been exhausted.

Using the Library Catalog

The computer or card catalog is an excellent tool for searching a library collection. It is not, however, to be used exclusive of all other indexes. Using the computer or catalog exclusively keeps students from valuable sources of information that are not listed in the catalog, such as information within periodicals, information within reference sources, and information within the books in the nonfiction collection. Unfortunately, many students do consider the catalog their only access to information in the library. This notion often leads to dissatisfaction, especially when they use limited subject headings. When they begin to think of the library as a whole, they are less likely to continue the exclusive use of the computer or catalog.

While the catalog is an excellent index to the titles in a library collection, it is also a guide to the sections of the library where general information on a topic can be located. Students can learn to use the catalog to locate a particular section and to survey the books in the section using indexes and tables of contents to locate bits of information. One student expressed his dissatisfaction with using the catalog to locate specific information on a focus: "The card catalog is never useful to me. In the public library, there's an 800's section. I don't know if that's true of all libraries. It has a lot of world plays and next to it, I saw books on the Theater of the Absurd and French literature." Students must understand that the library catalog can direct them to sections of the library as well as to titles in the library. As some experienced searchers have explained, "I find my number and look a little to the left and a little to the right."

There are two approaches to using the books, once the appropriate sections have been located. Students may survey the books and they may browse through the books. Surveying is the formal technique of checking the index for pages and the table of contents for chapters. Browsing is perusing and skimming the pages and chapters for pertinent information. A combination of the two approaches is useful for locating information in books. One student described finding information in the books on a shelf of the library: "I picked up every book on the shelf and looked under fantasy. I came across a couple of good ones. I came across one by Piaget by mistake which I was going to look up anyway." Students must learn to use the catalog creatively for the many different purposes their search requires.

Using Additional Access Points

Students must learn to consistently use a variety of access points to the library collection. One of the most frequently overlooked sources is the subject reference collection. Reference sources are listed in the computer or card catalog under broad subject headings. Specific information on a focus, however, must be located within reference books, through an index or other access point. Subject reference sources contain a wealth of information that is commonly unavailable in any of the other sources in the library. Students need to form the habit of consulting the reference collection on the subject that encompasses their topic in search of information pertaining to their focus.

Another essential access point to information is indexes in books in the nonfiction collection. Many students do not know how to locate information on their focus using indexes in books. Although they may have been instructed on indexes, many have had limited experience with actually using indexes. They have not become proficient at the skill and need further instruction and practice.

A third important source of information that is frequently overlooked because access is outside the computer or card catalog is periodicals. Every student should learn to use the periodical indexes. These indexes provide access to current information that is unavailable in any other form. Familiarity with the periodical indexes also acquaint students with the concept of indexing, which prepares them for using subject indexes such as *Social Sciences and Humanities Index, Art Index,* and *Public Affairs Information Service.* The indexes, while not commonly available in the media center, may be used in public or academic libraries. Before students leave secondary school, they should understand that indexing in various subjects provides access to current information that is not available in the book collection. They should also learn to use indexes to access information in other periodical sources in the library collection, such as *Facts on File, Social Issues Resource Service,* and the *New York Times.* Students should also have extensive experience using a CD-ROM index, such as *Wilsondisc* and *Infotrac.*

Predicting the Usefulness of Sources

As students become more familiar with the library collection, they can predict the sources that will be most useful for collecting information on a particular focus. They learn that periodicals are a useful source of current information and that introductions in works of fiction often include critical remarks. One student described his predictions of sources as he began collecting information: "Books about her life and about the success of her books, how much they grossed, were not useful. I was looking for books about her technique, not about her life or the production of her plays."

Students follow their predictions and test them for accuracy. As they become more experienced, they adjust their library search according to the accuracy of their predictions as to the usefulness of sources. If one type of source is not found to be useful, they learn to shift to another type of source rather than abandoning their search. This is how a student described changing tactics: "I expected biographies to have parts on what influenced his writing. But I found that biographies didn't help. So I looked up Hemingway in the card catalog and took down every number."

Directed Reading

Reading becomes more directed in the collection stage than in earlier stages of the research process. At this point, students must learn to seek only the most useful sources and to read only the most pertinent information. They need to concentrate their attention on their focus and to become highly selective in the information that they read. A student referred to directed reading used in collecting information on a focus as "serious reading." She said, "I usually sit by myself and read, but I don't do serious reading until the end."

Students may continue to be interested in the general information found on the topic. General information, however, can be distracting in the collection stage. If the task of collecting information is to be accomplished, students must read with their focus in mind. They must learn to skim the most useful sources for pertinent information. Pertinent information should be carefully read and recorded in notes.

Notetaking

Notetaking is an essential skill in collecting information. As students read about their focus, they need to record the ideas and facts they are planning to use in their paper or other presentation. Notetaking requires formal techniques but the mechanics of the task should never be made to seem more important than the purpose of the task.

Little research has been done on how people actually take notes. How do we choose what is to be written down and what is to be left out? Many students have difficulty deciding exactly what to take down in their notes. They frequently make the mistake of attempting to write down everything. They must learn some techniques to enable them to note that which will be needed when they are preparing their presentation.

There are two types of information that students need to record in their notes. The first type is direct quotations which they plan to use. The second is the ideas and facts they intend to present by paraphrasing and summarizing. The two types of information must be clearly differentiated from each other in the notes of students.

It is often difficult for students to discern between what should be quoted and what can be paraphrased. Students can learn to make a note of a quotation when they consider an author's wording essential for presenting a thought. Direct quotations must be copied down verbatim and enclosed in quotation marks.

Ideas and facts to be paraphrased can be noted in an outline, a list, or other short form. Every word need not be noted but the main ideas and significant facts on the focus should be recorded. Students sometimes mistakenly think that when they change a few words in an author's text, they do not need to identify the source in a footnote. They must learn to note and identify the source of all of the ideas and facts they plan to use, whether they will be quoted, paraphrased, or summarized.

Notetaking requires abstracting, which is a complex skill involving the highest level of thinking. Students must cull ideas and facts from a number of different sources and combine these with their own thoughts. The emphasis in notetaking should continue to be on the thoughts that students are building about the focus they plan to present. A student described taking notes on his focus in this way: "Then I researched and found as much as I could. I took down anything on 'the first person narrative.'"

While they are taking notes on the focus, some students are developing plans for presenting their focus. Two students described organizing their notes as they recorded them: The first student explained that, "As I read, my focal point didn't really change that much, maybe it became more concise. I knew what I was writing about and I took the information and added it to my outline." The other student said, "When I took notes, I took them in prose. When I found a quote, I put it with the theme it related to."

A systematic method of notetaking must be employed. Many teachers recommend the use of cards. They suggest complex ways to compile and organize the cards, commonly using elaborate systems of coding. Cards, however, can be cumbersome for students who are learning the research process. When cards are not required, students rarely use this method on their own. Most students use a notebook as they are accustomed to doing in other notetaking situations, such as class lectures and assigned reading. In this program of teaching the research process, the journal is used as a notebook for recording information on the focus during the information collecting stage. The journal pages are divided in half by folding them vertically. The bibliographic citation of the source is written at the top of the first page of notes. Each page of notes for that source may be numbered so that the complete citation does not have to be repeated on each page. On the left side of the page, the quotations and ideas of the author are noted. On the right side of the page, students may record their own reactions or additions to the author's ideas.

Notetaking is a necessary, formal technique for collecting information. The mechanics, however, must not overwhelm the development of thoughts. The emphasis in the information collecting stage of the research process should be placed squarely on the accumulation of ideas and thoughts about a research focus in preparation for presenting. Notetaking should enhance the development of thoughts about the focus.

Keeping Track of Sources

The source log, which was used in the exploration stage of the research process, can continue to be used while students are collecting information. A complete citation of every source used must be recorded in the log. In the description column, students can record the page in their journal where their notes on that particular source are located.

The source log is adequate for short papers up to ten pages with ten to twenty sources. For longer papers with more extensive use of sources, such as theses and dissertations, bibliography cards may be more appropriate. Once students learn the intricacies of bibliographic citation, they can easily transfer to bibliography cards. Secondary students, however, find the cards tedious, confusing, and easy to lose. The source log may be conveniently clipped in the journal notebook. They then have one notebook, which is easy to carry, use, and keep track of, for collecting information and noting citations. The computer is an excellent tool for keeping track of sources. Citations may be transferred from the notebook to a computer file.

Role of the Teacher

Even the most conscientious students need some direction in collecting information. Students new to library research tend to either copy directly from their sources or make sparse, inadequate notes of their readings. In the following statement, a student described the need for direction. "It didn't seem to me that I had really done research because I hadn't written a word yet. I had pages with two lines written on them from my readings. But I hadn't really written down my ideas."

Students need instruction in the proper form for citing the various types of library materials, such as books or periodical and encyclopedia articles. They can learn that there are several accepted forms of bibliographic citation, but one should be required for them to use consistently throughout the research assignment. A style manual should be recommended, which may be available in the media center if it is not possible to have one for each student. The form of citation of sources in bibliographies should be clearly differentiated from that used in footnotes or endnotes. Students commonly find the difference between the form used in footnotes and bibliographies confusing. The form for bibliographic citation should be learned first. Footnoting may be taught in the last stage of the research process when students are ready to write their papers.

Discussing their ideas about the focus continues to be helpful for students in clarifying and organizing their developing thoughts. Guided class discussion sessions may be provided during this stage.

Role of the Library Media Specialist

When students are collecting information about their focus, most have defined their topic sufficiently to enable them to request the information they need. This is when the librarian is found to be most helpful. Many students, however, misunderstand how the librarian can help them in their research process. Some want the librarian to locate the materials for them, while others consider requesting the librarian's assistance akin to cheating. Both attitudes get in the way of productive assistance. All library media specialists are familiar with the overly demanding student but many underdemanders slip by unnoticed.

Several students described having difficulty using libraries, but they did not seek the help of the librarian. They said, "I went to [the] library and I really didn't know where anything was." "When I went to [the library] I found a lot of books. There was one book that had Dickens in the index but I couldn't find him in the book. I looked for about 15 minutes but it was a waste of time, there was nothing on Dickens." "I looked in magazines and newspaper indexes. I wrote them all down but I didn't look up the magazines. I didn't use any of them. I had enough trouble finding them in the index. I stayed there so long I had a headache."

Students need instruction on when and how to ask reference questions, and can later acquire a degree of independence in using libraries. Competence in collecting information develops with an understanding of the organization of information in libraries and experience in using libraries. Teaching the research process involves presenting a broad perspective of information organization through classification and indexing along with extensive practice in collecting information in the media center.

The following activities are planned to assist students in collecting information related to their focus.

ACTIVITY 5-1
TIME LINE OF THE RESEARCH PROCESS

The time line helps students to visualize the total research process. It enables them to understand where they are in the process, to define the task before them, and to know what feelings to expect. The activity also helps students to gain a realistic sense of timing throughout the research process.

Time: 20 minutes

Materials: chalkboard

Note: This is an extension of Activity 1-5.

Conducted by: teacher or library media specialist

Activity Directions: Draw the time line of the research process on the chalkboard, labeling the first five stages as shown here.

receive assignment	select topic	explore for focus	form focus	collect information

Review the first four stages and briefly identify the fifth stage. You could say this: "You have received your assignment, selected a topic, explored for a focus, and formed a focus for your research. You are now ready to collect information about your focus." Point to the place on the time line that depicts the fifth stage.

Describe the task of the fifth stage in this way: "Your task at this stage is to locate information pertaining to your focus. You will need to read and take notes on the information that you plan to use in your presentation. You will need to gather information from many different kinds of materials in the library."

Describe the feeling that students are likely to experience in the fifth stage: "Most students feel more confident about their research at this point. Your focus gives you a sense of direction and an understanding of what information to look for. Many students also find that they become more interested in their topic as they collect information about it."

Remind students to form a focus before they enter this stage: "Be certain that you have a focus for your research before you begin to collect information. Collecting information involves taking notes. Take notes only on information that pertains to your focus."

Follow-up: This activity is intended to be followed by activities to help students collect information on a focus.

ACTIVITY 5-2
THINKING OF THE LIBRARY AS A WHOLE

This activity helps students consider how the various collections in a library can inform them about their topic. Students become aware of the patterns of information organization and are encouraged to use a number of different kinds of information.

Time: one class period (the writing may be given as a homework assignment)

Materials: Students may use their journals or Worksheet 5-2.

Conducted by: library media specialist or the teacher

Activity Directions: Explain that the library has a number of different collections, each containing a particular type of information. "When you are collecting information on a topic, you will need to refer to the different kinds of information that apply to your topic. As I describe each collection of the library, be thinking of the kind of information you might find that would be useful to your research.

"Reference—General reference such as encyclopedias, dictionaries, atlases, and almanacs have background information, definitions, and statistics that you may continue to need. Subject reference materials have information on the areas of knowledge that contain each topic. Basic information about your topic is presented in an objective way that helps to view information in nonfiction books from a broader perspective."

"Nonfiction—Much of your information will come from the nonfiction collection. Think about what you are looking for and what you hope to find. Remember that many of these books may present one author's point of view or may be about one aspect of the topic. Read carefully and critically."

"Biography—In most subjects, certain people have made a significant contribution or have been leaders. The biographies of these people offer an important source of information about a topic."

"Fiction—If your topic is about an author or a type of literature, the actual writing becomes a source that should not be overlooked. Also, fiction about your topic can offer a perspective that other material cannot. For example, a paper on the early history of labor unions may be enhanced by an acquaintance with *The Jungle* by Upton Sinclair."

"Periodical—Magazines and newspapers offer current information about your topic. In addition a retrospective topic may be examined in terms of its present impact."

"Vertical file—Pamphlets and periodical clippings are collected in the vertical file. The material varies in quality and significance but you may find some interesting information that is not otherwise accessible."

"Databases—There are many online or CD-ROM databases that contain statistical information, citations of periodical articles, or the text of the articles themselves. You may be able to find information here that is unavailable in any other way."

Have students write what they expect to find about their topic in each collection in the library. Urge them to be very specific. Circulate to offer assistance to individual students while they are writing.

Follow-up: In a subsequent class session, have students share their ideas about the information they expect to find by discussing their answers. Alert individual students to any type of material they may have been unaware of that might prove useful to them.

Name _____

Date _____

Topic _____

Focus _____

USING THE WHOLE LIBRARY COLLECTION

Describe how each type of information in the library collection can inform you about your research topic.

Reference

General

Subject

Biography

Nonfiction

Fiction

Periodicals

Magazines

Newspapers

Vertical File Materials

Computer Databases

© 1994 by Carol Collier Kuhlthau

Worksheet/Activity 5–2

ACTIVITY 5-3
FINDING DESCRIPTORS ALONG THE WAY

In Activity 3-2, students identified descriptors relating to their topics. They will need to identify additional descriptors leading to specific information on their focus. This activity helps students list descriptors specific to their focus.

Time: one class session (students are introduced to this activity in class and assigned to complete it outside class as they use library sources)

Materials: Students may use their journals or Worksheet 5-3.

Conducted by: library media specialist or teacher

Activity Directions: Have students turn to their list of descriptors developed in Activity 3-2. Explain that the descriptors may be used as subject headings to locate information about their general topic in the library catalog and other indexes. Have them look over the list and eliminate any that do not apply to their focus. Tell them: "You will need to list additional descriptors about your focus. As you learn more about your topic, you will encounter terms, people, events, and places that relate to your focus. Keep a list of these descriptors as you find them. They may be useful as subject headings to lead you to information in indexes in books, as well as the library catalog and periodical indexes."

Follow-up: As students are using indexes to locate information, remind them to refer to their list of descriptors for alternative subject headings.

Name _____

Date _____

Topic _____

Focus _____

FINDING DESCRIPTORS ALONG THE WAY

As you read about your topic, keep a list of descriptors that relate to your focus to use as subject headings.

1. Terms and key words

2. People

3. Places

4. Events

© 1994 by Carol Collier Kuhlthau

Worksheet / Activity 5–3

ACTIVITY 5-4
ALTERNATIVE SUBJECT HEADINGS

This activity acquaints students with the subject headings used in the library catalog and other indexes. They are urged to think of the general subject that contains their topic as well as more specific subject heading terms pertaining to their focus for locating library materials.

Time: one class period (this activity may be combined in one session with Activity 5-5, "Understanding Classification Hierarchy")

Materials: chalkboard

Conducted by: library media specialist with the teacher

Activity Directions: Explain that established subject headings are used in the catalog and descriptors are used in periodical indexes. Show students the *Sear's List of Subject Headings* or the Library of Congress list, and *Infotrac* or *Wilsondisc* printout, saying, "Sometimes the term you use is not the term in the catalog or index. You will need to use alternative subject headings.

"The purpose of subject headings is to bring all of the materials in the library collection together in the catalog. The purpose of the classification system is to bring materials on one subject together. For example, a book has only one classification number or call number, but it may be listed under more than one subject heading in the catalog. To locate all of the library materials that contain information on your topic, you will need to use as many subject headings as you can.

"Subject headings are usually printed in capital letters. Normally, materials are assigned the most specific subject heading. Subject headings are made more specific by adding adjectives, subdivisions, phrases, locations, time periods, etc." Demonstrate several examples on a chalkboard, such as Art, American; Insurance, Fire; Birds-Migration; United States-History-1861–1865.

"When you find the general subject heading, read the additions carefully to identify the ones that pertain to your topic." Distribute copies of "Alternative Subject Headings," Worksheet 5-4.

Remind students to use *see* and *see also* references for alternative subject headings. Define *see* and *see also* references in this way: "*See* references refer to the subject heading that is used in the index. *See also* references refer to other subject headings used in the index."

Explain that subject headings and descriptors for a topic are not necessarily the same. For example, *Sears* uses "WORD PROCESSING" while *Readers' Guide* uses "WORD PROCESSORS AND PROCESSING"; *Sear's* uses "HAZARDOUS WASTE" while *Readers' Guide* uses "HAZARDOUS SUBSTANCES."

Variation: You may want to have a copy of the *Sear's List of Subject Headings* and a printout from a computer index for students to refer to on a regular basis.

Follow-up: Encourage students to confer with the librarian when they are confused about what term to use for a subject heading.

© 1994 by Carol Collier Kuhlthau

Name _____

Date _____

Topic _____

Focus _____

ALTERNATIVE SUBJECT HEADINGS

The term you use to describe your topic may not be the same term used as a subject heading in the computer or card catalog. Use the *Sear's List of Subject Headings* to find the subject headings that are used in the catalog. List the subject headings that describe your topic. Look for your topic in a periodical index. List the descriptors you find.

1.

2.

3.

4.

5.

ACTIVITY 5-5
UNDERSTANDING CLASSIFICATION HIERARCHY

This activity helps students locate information on their topic using classification hierarchy. They learn that a hierarchical system for classifying information is the basis of both the Dewey Decimal System and the Library of Congress System of cataloging.

Time: one class period (this activity may be combined in one class session with Activity 5-4 "Alternative Subject Headings")

Materials: chalkboard or chart paper; Dewey Decimal Classification System and Library of Congress System Lists

Conducted by: library media specialist with the teacher

Activity Directions: Briefly describe the basic plan of a classification system, saying: "In a library all information is divided into general subject areas and subdivided from the broadest to the most specific categories. The Dewey Decimal System and the Library of Congress System are hierarchical systems of organizing information."

Distribute the lists which show the main categories of the two common library classification systems.

On a chalkboard or chart, demonstrate the subdivisions within one of the main classes of the Dewey Decimal System. For example:

600 Applied Sciences
630 Agriculture
636 Animal Husbandry
636.1 Horses
636.16 Ponies

or

500 Pure Sciences
590 Zoological Sciences
599 Mammals
599.2 Marsupials

"When you search for information on your topic, you will need to look for materials in the main categories as well as in the more specific subdivisions. You will miss information if you look only for materials that are specifically classified on your focused topic. You will probably not be able to find enough information if you do not also use materials classified in general categories.

"What is the main category in the Dewey Decimal System that contains your topic? What are the subdivisions within the main category that contain your topic? List the call numbers that may contain materials with information on your topic." (See Worksheet 5-5 for this activity.)

Variation: If students plan to use a library with the Library of Congress System, have them do the exercise for that system also.

Follow-up: Have students continue to use the classification system as they are collecting information. Encourage them to seek your assistance if they have further questions.

DEWEY DECIMAL CLASSIFICATION SYSTEM
TEN MAIN CLASSES AND SUBDIVISIONS

000—General Works
  010—Bibliographies
  020—Libraries
  030—Encyclopedias
  050—Periodicals
  060—General Organizations
  070—Journalism
  080—General Collections
  090—Rare Books

100—Philosophy
  110—Metaphysics
  120—Knowledge, Purpose of Man
  130—Supernatural, Parapsychology, Occult
  140—Philosophical Viewpoints
  150—Psychology
  160—Logic
  170—Ethics
  180—Ancient
  190—Modern

200—Religion
  220—Bible
  290—Comparative

300—Social Sciences
  320—Political Science
  330—Economics
  340—Law
  350—Public Administration
  360—Social Problems
  370—Education
  380—Commerce and Trade
  390—Customs and Folklore

400—Language
  410—Linguistics
  420—English
  430—German
  440—French
  450—Italian
  460—Spanish
  470—Latin
  480—Greek
  490—Other

500—Pure Sciences
  510—Mathematics
  520—Astronomy
  530—Physics
  540—Chemistry
  550—Earth Science
  560—Paleontology
  570—Life Sciences
  580—Botany
  590—Zoology

600—Technology
  610—Medical Sciences
  620—Engineering
  630—Agriculture
  640—Home Economics
  650—Business
  660—Chemical technology
  670—Manufactures
  690—Building

700—The Arts
  710—Landscape
  720—Architecture
  730—Sculpture
  740—Drawing and decorative
  750—Painting
  760—Prints and print making
  770—Photography
  780—Music
  790—Performing arts and recreation

800—Literature
  810—American
  820—English
  830—German
  840—French
  850—Italian
  860—Spanish
  870—Latin
  880—Greek
  890—Other

900—Geography and History
  910—Geography and travel
  920—Group Biography
  930—Europe
  950—Asia
  960—Africa
  970—North America
  980—South America
  990—Other

LIBRARY OF CONGRESS CLASSIFICATION SYSTEM
EIGHTEEN MAIN CLASSES

A   Generalities

B   Philosophy—Religion

C–F History

G   Geography

H   Social Science

J   Political Science

K   Law

L   Education

M   Music

N   Fine Arts

P   Language—Literature

Q   Science

R   Medicine

S   Agriculture

T   Technology

U   Military Science

V   Naval Science

Z   Bibliography

© 1994 by Carol Collier Kuhlthau

Name _____

Date _____

Topic _____

Focus _____

UNDERSTANDING CLASSIFICATION HIERARCHY

List the main category in the Dewey Decimal System that contains your topic.

List the subdivision within the main category that may contain your topic.

List the general call numbers that may contain material on your topic.

ACTIVITY 5-6
USING THE LIBRARY CATALOG

This activity guides students in using the computer or card catalog to locate materials on their focus. They learn to use alternative subject headings. They decide on which materials to locate by reading the bibliographic and descriptive information in the catalog.

Time: one class session (students may need to complete the activity outside of class)

Materials: the media center catalog and collection; search logs (see Activity 3-5)

Conducted by: library media specialist with teacher

Activity Directions: Using their list of descriptors from Activity 5-3, have students look up all of the subject headings in the library catalog. Direct them to read each citation carefully to determine if the material relates to their focus. Request that they log all of the sources pertaining to their focus in their source logs. They must notice whether the material is a circulation book, reference material, or an audio-visual and use the appropriate source log. In addition, have students note whether circulating materials are in nonfiction, biography, or fiction collections.

Briefly review the information contained in a citation, stressing that in addition to the bibliographic information, the citation may indicate the inclusion of illustrations, bibliography, indexes, and descriptions of contents. Explain that this information can help them assess the usefulness of the material. Alert them to the importance of using copyright dates to assess the accuracy and currency of information.

Follow-up: Collect and evaluate the source logs. Recommend subject headings, collections, and sources that may have been overlooked.

ACTIVITY 5-7
BROWSING THE SHELVES

In this activity students locate books on the library shelves. They find information pertaining to their focus by using the index and the table of contents in the books.

Note: This activity was designed to follow Activity 5-6.

Time: one class session (Students will probably need to continue further investigation on their own. This may be combined in the same class session as 5-6. However, caution should be taken not to rush students through either activity.)

Materials: media center collection; source logs (books); list of descriptors

Conducted by: library media specialist with the teacher

Activity Directions: Have students identify and mark each source on the source log (books) as nonfiction, biography, and fiction. Explain that the call number indicates the section in which each source belongs. Remind them where each section is located in the media center.

Direct students to locate the books on the shelves and use the indexes within the books to determine which have information pertaining to their focus. Briefly review the procedure for finding information on topics using an in-book index. Recommend that students refer to their list of descriptors for subject headings when locating information in book indexes. Tell them: "Use the descriptors that most specifically depict your focus. General descriptors led you to the book but specific descriptors will lead you to the information on your focus within the book. Look for books that have several pages on your focus, preferably consecutive pages."

Describe the difference between using an index and using a table of contents to locate information on a topic. "The table of contents lists the titles of the chapters in the book. This is sometimes useful for locating an entire chapter on your focus. Check both the table of contents and the index."

Explain the use of browsing. "Many experienced library researchers use a technique called browsing to help them find information. After you have obtained the call number from the catalog and have located the books on the library shelves, you also look at the books in the same vicinity to see if they contain information on your focus. This is a useful technique when you are having difficulty locating sufficient material. The books are classified by subject content and those in the vicinity of your call number may also contain some information pertaining to your topic." (See Worksheet 5-7 for this Activity.)

Recommend that they choose books that pertain to their focus and check out those they intend to use. Have students note if the book is useful, not useful, or not available in the description column of the source log.

Circulate and offer individual assistance. Encourage students to ask for help if they experience difficulty. Initiate offers of assistance to students who seem reluctant to seek help or are straying from the task.

Follow-up: Urge students to return to the media center to continue locating information and to seek your assistance when needed.

© 1994 by Carol Collier Kuhlthau

Name _____

Date _____

Topic _____

Focus _____

BROWSING THROUGH MATERIALS ON THE SHELVES

1. List the call numbers you have recorded in your source log.

2. Locate the section where most of the call numbers are located. Find information on your focus by using the indexes in the books.

   Source title   Page

3. Find information on your focus by using the table of contents.

   Source title   Chapter and page

4. Look at the table of contents and indexes of other books in the same vicinity of the call numbers. Add any new sources to your source log.

   Source title   Page

5. Categorize each source in your source log as most useful, useful, or least useful, based on what you found in the index and table of contents.

Worksheet / Activity 5–7

ACTIVITY 5-8
USING THE REFERENCE COLLECTION

This activity provides opportunities for students to use subject and general reference sources. They become aware of the kinds of information they can expect to find in reference sources within the context of their particular research focus.

Time: one class session (students probably will need additional time outside of class to complete the activity)

Materials: the reference collection in the media center; source log (reference); list of descriptors

Conducted by: library media specialist with teacher

Activity Directions: Explain that many reference sources are frequently overlooked by students. You may use this explanation: "You have been using general reference sources, such as encyclopedias and dictionaries, to get background information and to define your topic. There are also encyclopedias and dictionaries and other reference books in the subject area that encompasses your topic." Remind students that reference sources are not limited to books. They will want to consult electronic reference sources, such as *Facts on File News Digest* and *Grolier's Electronic Encyclopedia*.

Describe how to locate information in subject reference sources: "Subject reference sources are usually arranged by alphabetical order and most have an index. You will need to examine each source to determine how the contents are arranged. Do not hesitate to ask for help if you are confused about how to use the reference source."

Have students locate the reference books they have listed on their source logs. (See worksheet 5-8.) In addition, recommend that they browse through other sources in the same section of the reference collection. Urge them to use their list of descriptors as subject headings Remind students of the circulation policy in the media center. They may need to plan to use reference material in the library. Tell students: "You will need to identify the information you plan to use and set aside time to spend in the media center for reading and taking notes. Reference sources are intended to be referred to, not to be read all the way through. You will probably find that the information you need can be read and noted in a relatively short period of time."

Alert students to general reference sources that may have information essential to their research, for example, almanacs for statistics, and atlases for maps and geographical information. Also make them aware of the biographical sources in the reference collection that might have information pertaining to their research focus.

Circulate among the students, assisting individuals to locate and use reference sources.

Variation: If the research assignment falls within one subject area, give a survey of the reference sources relating to that subject. For example, if the research assignment is related to literature, describe the sources of literary criticism and literary biography in the reference collection.

Follow-up: Encourage students to return to the media center to use reference sources on their own time. Offer assistance when needed.

Name _____

Date _____

Topic _____

Focus _____

USING THE REFERENCE COLLECTION

1. Write the call number of reference materials you found in the library catalog and have listed in your source log.

   Call number _____

2. Check the Dewey Decimal or Library of Congress Classification listing for the main class containing your topic.

   Main class _____

3. Using the call numbers, locate the section of the reference collection that relates to your topic. Look through the reference books, using the index and table of contents to locate information on your topic.

   Source title   Page

4. Search an online database for additional information relating to your topic.

   Source title   Location

5. Add to your source log any useful reference sources that you find.

Worksheet/Activity 5–8

© 1994 by Carol Collier Kuhlthau

ACTIVITY 5-9
USING CURRENT SOURCES OF INFORMATION

This activity provides opportunities for students to use newspapers, magazines, and vertical file materials. They learn to use the indexes to these sources within the context of their own research focus.

Time: one class session (students probably will need additional time outside of class to complete the activity)

Materials: the media center collection; source log (periodicals) to be filled in during this session; list of descriptors

Conducted by: library media specialist with the teacher

Preparation: Students who are unfamiliar with periodical indexes will need to learn how to use an index prior to this activity.

Activity Directions: Explain that libraries have collections of current information such as magazines, newspapers, and pamphlets: "These sources contain information on current findings, opinions, and happenings that can make a research topic more timely and interesting. For some current topics, most of the information will be in periodicals. For historical research, periodicals will not be as useful, but you may find an article that brings a current perspective to a retrospective topic."

Describe the current information sources in the media center and explain how to locate information in these sources. "To find information in current sources you will need to use indexes. The *Readers' Guide to Periodical Literature* and electronic indexes, such as *Wilsondisc* and *Infotrac* will lead you to magazine articles on your focus. *Facts on File* and *Editorials on File* are sources of newspaper articles excluding the *New York Times*. The *New York Times Index* and the *National Newspaper Index* are sources of newspaper articles. *Social Issues Resource Service* (SIRS) contains magazine and journal articles on various areas of current concern. Some of the articles are included in the volume with the index such as *Facts on File* and *SIRS*. Others are indexes to articles in the periodical collection of the media center or other library. Explain that although all have subject access, each has location symbols that are unique to that index. Briefly explain how to use each index.

Explain that periodicals report on an event at the time that it occurred: "Back issues, such as those compiled in the *New York Times School Collection,* are an excellent source of primary material and information in the tone and the setting of the time that an event happened." Vertical file material may be introduced with periodical material.

Have students use the indexes and record the articles that they plan to use in their source log (periodicals). (See Worksheet 5-9.) Assist students individually in using the indexes to locate information on their focus. Urge them to use their list of descriptors as subject headings.

Variation: Introduce advanced students to indexes to subjects such as *Social Sciences Index, Humanities Index, Art Index,* and *Public Affairs Information Service.* If these are not available in the media center collection, refer students to public libraries and academic libraries to use the indexes.

Follow-up: Encourage students to return to the media center to use current sources. Offer assistance when needed.

© 1994 by Carol Collier Kuhlthau

Name _____

Date _____

Topic _____

Focus _____

USING CURRENT SOURCES OF INFORMATION

Locate information on your topic in each of the following indexes. State the volume and page that contains information on your topic.

	Volume	Page
Newspapers		
Facts on File		
Editorials on File		
New York Times Index		
National Newspaper Index		
other		
Magazines		
Readers' Guide to Periodical Literature		
Social Issues Resource Service		
other		
Pamphlets		
Vertical File		
other		

Check each of the indexes above and record bibliographic citations in your source log (periodical).

ACTIVITY 5-10
EVALUATING SOURCES

This activity helps students select materials that will contribute information to their research. They learn to consider the original purpose of library materials and also the date of publication, perspective of the author, and the type and scope of the presentation.

Time: 40 minutes or one class period

Materials: chalkboard

Conducted by: library media specialist with the teacher

Activity Directions: On a chalkboard or chart, list the following different types of sources of information in a library collection: newspapers, magazines, vertical file materials, nonfiction, fiction, encyclopedias, other reference sources.

Explain that few library materials are written especially for a library collection but are originally prepared for other purposes. Here's one way to explain the idea: "To select information for your research, you will find it helpful to consider the original purpose of the materials you are using. For example, information in periodicals is current and quickly becomes outdated. Information in a nonfiction book may present only one aspect of a topic or one particular point of view."

In a discussion, have the students describe the original purpose of each of the sources listed. (See Worksheet 5-10.) For example:

Newspapers: daily reporting and commentary of news events.

Magazines: weekly or monthly reporting and commentary of news, life-styles, and special interest.

Vertical file materials: randomly collected clippings and pamphlets of inconsistent value and a variety of purposes, such as advertising or public information.

Nonfiction: factual information and summaries, as well as reports and commentaries, often presenting one aspect of a topic or one particular point of view.

Fiction: literature of an author intended for a following of readers.

Encyclopedias: a compilation of what is generally known, original purpose is for reference use, such as inclusion in library collection.

Other reference materials: a compilation of what is generally known within a subject area or a type of format such as maps or statistics; unlike other library materials, reference materials are intended for library collections.

Tell students: "Think about how you can use each type of material to collect information on your topic."

Explain the difference between primary and secondary sources, saying: "Primary sources consist of autobiographies, journals, historical documents, letters, novels, plays, and interviews. Secondary sources consist of information about the topic by authorities in the field that are found in most of the materials in the reference and the nonfiction sections of the media center." Encourage students to seek both kinds of sources.

Some additional questions for students to consider when they use library materials are:

> When was the material published?
>
> Is the author presenting a particular point of view?
>
> Does the work present an overview of the topic or one aspect?
>
> What type of writing, such as essays based on opinion, factual account based on research, or a personal narrative based on experience, is presented in the material?

Follow-up: Urge students to locate information from each type of source that will be useful for their research. Assist them when they experience difficulty.

EVALUATING SOURCES

Five questions to consider in determining the value of the sources that you locate in the library:

1. What was the original purpose of the source?

2. When was the material published?

3. Is the author presenting a particular point of view?

4. Does the work present an overview of the topic or one aspect?

5. What type of writing, such as essays based on opinion, factual account based on research, or personal narrative based on experience, is presented in the material?

© 1994 by Carol Collier Kuhlthau

ACTIVITY 5-11
NOTETAKING

This activity provides students with a systematic method for taking notes from library materials. They learn to be selective in what they note by identifying the information they intend to quote, paraphrase, or summarize.

Time: one class period with additional time outside of class to continue collecting information by taking notes

Materials: materials on students' focused topics from the media center collection; journals or note sheets

Conducted by: teacher with the library media specialist

Activity Directions: Explain to students that they will need to take notes on information they intend to use in their presentation. Remind them to take notes only on information that relates directly to their focused topic. They may use their journals as notebooks for recording the information they are collecting.

You may wish to use this statement to explain notetaking: "As you take notes you will need to determine how you intend to present the information. Information may be presented by quoting, paraphrasing, or summarizing. Most information will be presented by paraphrasing or summarizing. Quotations are used only when you consider an author's wording essential for presenting the information.

"Paraphrasing is retelling the information in your own words. Summarizing is presenting the central meaning of the information in abbreviated form. Quoting is using the exact wording of the text to present the information. Ideas and facts that you intend to paraphrase or summarize can be noted in an outline or a list using key words and phrases. Quotations must be recorded verbatim and enclosed in quotation marks."

Have students divide their journal pages in half by folding vertically or provide them with note sheets. (See Worksheet 5-11.) Then say: "Write the citation of the source at the top of the sheet. On the left side of the page, note the quotations and the other information you intend to paraphrase and summarize. Record the page number of the source in the left margin beside each bit of information noted. On the right side of the paper, record your own reactions and additions to the information noted. Also note connections to information you have taken from other sources."

Follow-up: Assist students who have difficulty taking notes. Collect and read the notes. Work individually with students who need extra help.

NOTE SHEET

Author _____

Title _____

Place _____

Publisher _____

Date _____

Page	Quotations, facts, ideas	Your reactions and additions

© 1994 by Carol Collier Kuhlthau

STAGES OF THE
LIBRARY RESEARCH PROCESS:

Section 6
Preparing to Present

TASK	To conclude search for information.
THOUGHTS	Identify need for any additional information • Consider time limit • Notice decreasing relevance • Notice increasing redundancy • Exhaust resources.
FEELINGS	Sense of relief • Sometimes satisfaction • Sometimes disappointment.
ACTIONS	Recheck sources for information initially overlooked • Confirm information and bibliographic citations • Organize notes • Make outline • Write rough draft • Write final copy with footnotes and bibliography.
STRATEGIES	Return to library to make summary search.

SECTION 6

Preparing to Present

TASK OF THE SIXTH STAGE

In the sixth stage of the research process, students need to complete their library search, organize the notes they have taken, and prepare to present the findings of their library research. The findings may be presented in a research paper or in some other format as originally described in the research assignment.

When students enter the last stage of the research process, the main portion of their library research has been completed. However, they will often need to return to the library to make a final survey to be sure they have not overlooked significant sources. Many students find that they need to verify a citation of a source they have used or to confirm a particular fact or idea. However, most library searching is finished by the beginning of this stage.

The notes that have been taken must be reread and organized. Students will need to identify several main points around which to organize what they have recorded in their notes. An outline may be made of the main points and related information may be added to the outline as the notes are reread. In this way, students build a framework for presenting their findings about the focus of their topic.

The outline provides a structure for writing the research paper. The focus should be stated in an introduction. The ideas and facts in the student's notes provide the information for writing the body of the paper. The paper is completed by a summary paragraph containing a conclusive statement about the focus.

Students should not find it necessary to identify a focus at this stage. Their focus should have been formed before they began to collect information and further refined and adapted while the information was being collected. Students' notes should not be filled with extraneous information that they will not use in their presentation. Their notes should contain the ideas and facts about the focus that will be presented in their paper.

Feelings of Students While Preparing to Present

At the close of the research process, many students experience a sense of relief. Several students described their feelings in these ways: "Relief, the hard part is over, the easy part is coming. I find it a lot easier to write it out than to find information." "Relief, I'm finished, now just write." "Great, the hard part is over.

I'm almost done now. By the time I'm done with my search, I pretty much know what my paper is going to be like."

Other students dread writing the paper and do not experience a sense of relief until that task is completed: "You know that you have all of this information that you have to push into a report. I think that is the harder part. It's the least enjoyable."

Some students experience a feeling of dissatisfaction at this point in the research process. They are disappointed at not having found the information they were seeking or not having time to pursue a new lead that had opened up: "I felt that time was short. I started to get a real idea of the things I wanted to do. I felt I needed more information and that bothered me because I knew I didn't have time. I was angry with myself for not starting earlier."

Other students have a feeling of accomplishment at the close of the research process. They have learned about their topic. They have presented their findings in an acceptable form. They have successfully completed a difficult, complex task.

Completing Library Research

Students can determine that library research has been completed in a number of ways: (1) They have used the time allotted for the research assignment; (2) all useful sources have been exhausted; and (3) sufficient effort has been put forth. In many cases, running short of time becomes the controlling factor for students. However, when all three factors are given careful consideration, library research is more likely to be completed rather than merely stopped.

Keeping Within the Time Frame

Library research is commonly ended shortly before the research assignment is due. Rarely do students complete their use of the library ahead of time. The nature of library research makes the student want to return for "just one more bit of information" and to keep the search open as long as possible. Therefore, the time element is important for drawing library research to a close. Here's the way some students explained how time influenced them: "Usually the end of the search is made by the due date." "I was running out of time. . . ." "The end of the search is when time is up." "Because of lack of time, I stopped searching. I never really have a last source. I know it's time to write when the paper is due."

Time allotted for a complex research assignment, such as one requiring writing a research paper, can be anywhere from four to ten weeks. Most students who have had experience with research papers preferred a four-week time frame. They said: "He gave us a month and a half. I think the more time you have, the more you procrastinate. I think three or four weeks is best." "We had too much time. It was better when he gave us just a month. You don't need two months."

Students can learn to pace themselves in the research process to enable them to work their way through each stage effectively. Ability in pacing comes through experience and self-awareness in the research process.

Exhausting Resources

Students determine that they have located most of the useful resources in the library on their focus by encountering sources either of decreasing relevance or of increasing redundancy.

One student described her experience with encountering sources of diminishing relevance in this way: "You get to what you want and then afterwards start getting off the topic a little." Students can learn to recognize decreasing relevance in library sources. Of course, they must first have located and collected a substantial amount of relevant information on their focus. Diminishing relevance occurs only after the most useful sources in the library have been located and used.

Redundancy also occurs only after extensive use of library materials. When students begin to discover similar information in new sources, it signals the completion of their library research. One student described her experience with redundancy: "In the end you are just looking for extra things so you are sure you have everything. But a lot of it is repeat."

Knowing when library sources have been exhausted by recognizing signs of decreasing relevance and of increasing redundancy is a subtle technique that requires experience and practice. Students need patience, concentration, and determination to see a research project through to the end. They can learn to end library research because they have exhausted the available resources rather than merely stopping because time has run out.

Making a Sufficient Effort

Some students feel they have accomplished the research task if they have made what they consider a sufficient effort. They do not determine the completion of their library research solely on the adequacy of their findings. One student described this attitude in this way: "I get so sick and tired of digging through books that I say, 'This is good enough. I have done a good enough job. The material I have gotten is sufficient.'"

Students' estimation of sufficient effort does not necessarily match the effort required to complete researching a focus in the library. When students become accustomed to the considerable effort required in library research, they can more accurately judge when they have put forth sufficient effort. The amount of effort must be considered in relation to the information that has been collected on the focus and the requirements of the assignment.

Making a Final Check of the Library

Many students make a final check of the library collection before closing their research. They search for any source they might have overlooked. One student said: "I went back to the reference collection to check if there was anything I had missed. There was nothing I had missed. It wasn't in-depth and wasn't helpful." Another said: "When I think I have exhausted all of the books,

I may go to the library one more time to make sure I got everything I might want to get. I take the books again and I look through the index to make sure I didn't miss anything. Once I am sure that I have gotten everything I can, I am done."

Continuing library research for a short time after the most useful resources have been found is an important strategy for students to learn. Many students have a tendency to stop when they locate a few useful sources. These students may be missing valuable information by closing their research prematurely. Library research should be considered completed only when students begin to find less useful sources. As one student put it, "After I found what I wanted, I kept on looking. I stopped my search when I couldn't find anything else or when I was finding things that were getting me off track."

Adequately Supporting the Focus

At the completion of library research, the collected information should adequately present the focus to meet the requirements of the assignment. Students must learn to determine the extent and depth of their library research in terms of the requirements of the research assignment.

Having the focus clearly in mind is important for determining when library research is completed. Students who do not have a focus collect information on a general topic, and have difficulty concluding their library research. The amount of information available often becomes overwhelming and the research must be stopped rather than completed. Seeking information to support and build a focus provides manageable limits for library research. The focus also provides the center for organizing the information collected.

Organizing the Notes

When the library research has been completed, students must organize their notes in preparation for writing the research paper or making another type of presentation. Before they begin, it is helpful to state the focus in writing so that it is clearly in mind. Next, they should ask themselves what they want to say about the focus.

The first step in organizing notes is to read through all of the information that has been taken down and identify three to five main points about the focus in what has been recorded. The focus should encompass each of the main points that have been identified. Students should skim their notes with the main points in mind to be certain they have not overlooked a central point they want to include.

Next, students need to decide the order in which they will present the main points about the focus. After they have made the decision, the main points should be listed and numbered in the order in which they will be presented. They can read through their notes once again to determine the ideas and facts that are related to the main points. The ideas and facts can be numbered to correspond with the main point they describe.

Outlining

When students have identified the main points about the focus and the corresponding descriptive facts and ideas, they are ready to make an outline. The outline is composed of a detailed listing of topics and subtopics; in other words, main points and descriptive facts and ideas. An outline is a plan for presenting the findings on the focus. By constructing an outline, students are able to order their thoughts for writing.

Students can identify illustrations and examples in their notes and add them to the appropriate places in the outline. They may decide on what direct quotations they plan to use and add them to the outline. Information that will be paraphrased and summarized may be noted in the outline. Students' thoughts that extend and connect the information collected in the library research may also be indicated in the outline. Thus, the outline provides the planned structure for the research paper.

Quoting, Paraphrasing, and Summarizing

The information that students have collected in their notes can be quoted, paraphrased, and summarized to present the focus. The sources of each quotation, paraphrase, or summary must be identified in a footnote.

Information that students plan to quote directly should be written verbatim and enclosed in quotation marks. Quotations should be chosen to give the paper power and authority. Students can learn how to choose quotations and to use them sparingly since an overabundance of quotations diminishes their impact. Quotations should be used only when the author's wording contributes significantly to a student's presentation.

Most of the information in students' notes should be paraphrased or summarized. Paraphrasing is the complex skill of restating an author's idea in the student's own words. Students who have little past experience with paraphrasing are often tempted merely to substitute a few words here and there. Paraphrasing, however, requires thinking through the author's statement to comprehend it thoroughly and restating it clearly, using terms and phrases that are more familiar to the student.

Students must summarize some of the information in their notes or their presentations will be too long. Summarizing requires the ability to see what is central to an idea and to present it more succinctly. Paraphrasing and summarizing are complex skills that must be learned and practiced. It is helpful for students to have extensive experience with paraphrasing and summarizing before they need to use the skills in a library research assignment.

Connecting and Extending

In addition to presenting what they have researched in library materials, students must present their own ideas through connections and extensions. They need to make connections between the various ideas they are presenting in order to produce a meaningful whole. They also need to include their own ideas about the focus, extending what they have read in library materials.

Without connecting thoughts, a presentation is merely a group of disparate ideas and facts. The connections that students make link the ideas together. They need to decide the order in which the ideas are to be presented and to connect the various points.

Extensions are the insights and opinions that students develop about their topic. By extending what they have researched in the library, they develop a point of view on their topic. The introduction and the conclusion of the presentation includes students' extensions.

Writing the Paper

Writing the research paper is not part of the research process. In most cases, the research process is completed when the writing begins. This book does not attempt to include complete directions and activities to guide students through the writing as there are many books available on writing research papers. The writing instruction, however, should continue in the invitational tone recommended in this book.

The research paper is a compilation of the essential facts and ideas on a topic that have been culled from a variety of library sources. The information collected about a subject is presented from the students' perspective. They choose the information to present and the order of the presentation. In this way, a research paper is an original, creative presentation of a familiar body of information.

The findings of library research may be presented in a variety of ways. A debate, an oral report, or a slide/tape show are all alternatives to the research paper, with writing involved in the preparation for *any* presentation. The research paper, however, has a formal structure that sets it apart from other modes of presenting library findings.

The research paper is made up of an introduction, a body, and a conclusion. In the introduction, students state and describe the focus they have chosen. The body of the paper is composed of the findings of their library research, which describe and support the focus. Students select the main points, which they present through quoting, paraphrasing, and summarizing the sources they have read and taken notes on. The conclusion is a summary statement of their perspective on the focus.

There is a specific format for a research paper. Recommend a style manual for students to follow in writing and documenting their papers. They can learn that there are a number of acceptable forms, but that one should be chosen to be followed consistently throughout the paper. They will need to refer to the style manual for the form of footnotes and bibliography as well as structural elements, such as the title page, typing format, pagination, and quotations.

Students need to learn to write their papers in two main stages—the rough draft and the final copy. The rough draft, a working copy composed from their outline, is developed with quotations, paraphrasing, and summaries from their notes. (The teacher may review the rough draft to recommend revisions.) The final paper should be submitted neatly typed or handwritten with proofreading and editing revisions completed.

Footnotes

One of the unique features of a research paper is the necessity to cite sources of information in footnotes or endnotes. Occasionally, students are confused about the purpose of footnotes. The footnotes they are most familiar with are those in textbooks. Notes in textbooks serve to extend the information in the text and give definitions as well as identifying sources. Students frequently misunderstand the function of footnotes in a research paper because of their prior experience with notes in textbooks. They must clearly understand that the purpose of using footnotes in a research paper is to identify the sources of the quotations, paraphrasing, and summaries that they use and that these sources must be identified to avoid plagiarism.

Some students become so aware of the necessity to use footnotes that the mechanics of the research paper take precedence over the content. Here's how one student explained the way footnoting affected his choice of information in the research process: "It was a very good feeling when I finally hit on a critic who suggested what I said. That was a good feeling because I could use that. I could footnote it and that is exactly what I had to do. The teacher wanted to teach us how to do footnotes." Students must be aware that they need to identify the sources of information in their research paper. They should not be led to believe that the purpose of library research is to build up a series of footnotes.

To avoid placing undue emphasis on the use of footnotes, the technique and form of footnoting should not be taught at the beginning of the research process. Only the concept of using footnotes and a bibliography to avoid plagiarism should be presented at the beginning of the research process. The specific format to be used in footnoting, however, should be taught when students are preparing to write the research paper and are ready to use footnotes.

Bibliography

Students should have kept a record of the bibliographic citation of the sources they use throughout the research process. A recommended form of bibliographic citation should be introduced early in the research process. In this book, listing sources is introduced in the third stage when students are beginning to explore information on their topic. A log is provided for students to record library sources as they use them.

Recommend a style manual for students to follow consistently throughout the research assignment. They should also understand that there is more than one acceptable form of bibliographic citation. An acquaintance with several forms enables them to adapt more readily to whatever form is required in a future research assignment.

Students are often confused by the difference in the form of a footnote and the form of a citation in a bibliography. At this stage, they should learn to distinguish between the two and to refer to the recommended style manual when they are in doubt of the proper form to use.

The citations of the sources that have been listed in the source log must be selected and arranged to be included in the bibliography of the research paper. Rarely is every source that has been listed in the log included in the bibliography of the paper. Students need to select the sources of information that they actually used to present the focus in their research paper. The sources must be arranged alphabetically. This may be done by numbering the selected sources in the order in which they will appear in the bibliography and then by compiling the list according to the numbers assigned to each item.

Students can become confused about the way to cite different types of sources. Even those students who have had prior instruction and experience in listing sources in a bibliography may need to review the proper form. However, they should learn not to rely on their memory for the proper form of bibliographic citation but to make a habit of referring to a style manual.

Role of the Teacher

The teacher plays an important role in helping students learn how to prepare a presentation of their research. Students need guidance in organizing their notes and in constructing an outline of the information they have collected. The teacher should review students' plans for writing before they begin composing the rough draft. At this early stage of writing, the teacher can help students clarify their ideas for presentation.

Students also need guidance in learning how to select and use quotations. Deciding what information to quote, what to present by paraphrasing, and what to summarize is difficult for secondary students. They also need instruction with their own interpretations. Teachers can provide opportunities for both instruction and practice for students to learn these complex skills. Teachers of writing can guide students through the actual process of presenting the information and expressing their thoughts in a written research paper.

Role of the Library Media Specialist

Students need guidance in learning the difference between completing library research and merely stopping because they have run out of time. The library media specialist can help them recognize increasing redundancy and decreasing relevance in their library research. The library media specialist can also assist students in determining what is missing in the information they have gathered and guide them in finding sources to complete their library research. Students need to learn how to make a final check of the library collection to be certain they have not overlooked an important source.

The following activities help students prepare to present their library research findings.

ACTIVITY 6-1
ADEQUATELY SUPPORTING THE FOCUS

In this activity, students consider if the information they have collected is adequate to present their focus. They need to judge the amount of information they have collected with the requirements of the assignment.

Time: one class period (This activity may be combined in a session with Activity 6-2 and Activity 6-3.)

Materials: students' notes of information collected

Conducted by: teacher

Activity Directions: Explain to students that at the close of their library research, they will need to have collected sufficient information to present their findings within the requirements of the research assignment. Have one of the students read the research assignment aloud so that it will be fresh in their minds.

Direct students to reread their notes, thinking of the original assignment and also the focus they intend to present: (See Worksheet 6-1.) Ask them, "Does the information you have collected accomplish both purposes?"

Have students place a check beside any statements that need further information. Also have them write questions that remain unexplored.

Explain that the statements and questions may indicate a need for more information. Remind them that research projects usually leave some questions unexplored at their close. You might say: "Keep the original research assignment in mind as you are drawing your library research to a close. Be certain you have met the requirements of the assignment."

Follow-up: Invite students to confer with you if they need further direction in determining the adequacy of the information they have collected.

© 1994 by Carol Collier Kuhlthau

Name ⎯⎯⎯⎯⎯⎯⎯⎯⎯⎯⎯⎯

Date ⎯⎯⎯⎯⎯⎯⎯⎯⎯⎯⎯⎯

Topic ⎯⎯⎯⎯⎯⎯⎯⎯⎯⎯⎯

Focus ⎯⎯⎯⎯⎯⎯⎯⎯⎯⎯⎯

ADEQUATELY SUPPORTING THE FOCUS

Questions to consider as you read through your notes:

1. Does the information you have collected meet the requirements of the assignment? Explain your answer.

2. Is the information you have collected adequate for presenting your focus? Explain your answer.

3. What questions remain unanswered in the information collected?

4. Which of these questions are essential for presenting the focus and meeting the requirements of the assignment?

5. Which of these questions should be left for another research project?

Worksheet / Activity 6—1

ACTIVITY 6-2
SIGNS OF COMPLETING LIBRARY RESEARCH

Students learn to recognize increasing redundancy and decreasing relevance as signs that their library research is drawing to a close. They are urged to seek these signs rather than merely stopping because they have run out of time or have put forth what they consider sufficient effort.

Time: one class period (may be combined with Activity 6-3)

Materials: source logs

Conducted by: library media specialist with the teacher

Activity Directions: Explain to students that one way to determine if their library research is completed is when they have located the most useful sources of information on their topic in the library collection. (See Worksheet for this activity.) You might tell them: "It is not always easy to know when you have located the most useful sources but there are some signs to help you. One is increasing redundancy and another is decreasing relevance."

Define increasing redundancy in this way. "Increasing redundancy is apparent when the new sources you locate contain information similar to that of the sources you have already used. You begin to find less new information and more restatement of what you have previously collected."

Define decreasing relevance in this way: "Decreasing relevance is apparent when the new sources you locate contain less information pertaining to your focused topic. You begin to find information that is off the subject and less useful to your research."

Remind students not to stop their library research when they have found a few useful sources. Urge them to go beyond the most useful sources until they meet signs of increasing redundancy and decreasing relevance.

Have students assess the usefulness of the sources they have listed in their source log. Tell students: "Mark *useful, most useful,* or *least useful* next to each source. The last sources you located should be less useful and show decreasing relevance and increasing redundancy."

Follow-up: Urge students to continue their library research beyond locating a few useful sources.

Name _____

Date _____

Topic _____

Focus _____

SIGNS OF COMPLETING LIBRARY RESEARCH

Questions you should consider to help you know when you have located the most useful sources of information on your topics in the library collection:

1. Does the new source contain information similar to that in a source that I have previously used?

2. Does the new source contain little new information and much restatement of what I have previously collected?

3. Does the new source contain little information pertaining to my focus?

4. Does the new source contain information that is off the subject and is less useful to my research?

© 1994 by Carol Collier Kuhlthau

ACTIVITY 6-3
MAKING A FINAL CHECK OF THE LIBRARY

In this activity, students make a final check of the library collection before closing their research. They search for any sources they may have overlooked.

Time: one class period (may be combined with Activity 6-2)

Materials: media center collection; source logs

Conducted by: library media specialist with the teacher

Activity Directions: Explain to students that when they are closing their library research, it is helpful to make a final check of the library collection to be certain that important sources have not been overlooked.

Recommend that they check at least three places: the reference collection, the library catalog, and the periodical index. (See Worksheet 6-3.) Say, "Now that you are better informed on your focused topic and have an idea of how you will present your findings, you might find that a source you had previously considered irrelevant is useful to you after all. Make a final check to be sure that you have not overlooked some important, relevant information."

After students have checked the library collection, urge them to confer with the librarian. Check students' source logs and recommend any additional sources that they might find useful.

Follow-up: After students have made their final check of the library collection, you may want to check the source logs again to be certain they have included all major sources of information pertinent to their topics.

© 1994 by Carol Collier Kuhlthau

Name ———————————————

Date ———————————————

Topic ———————————————

Focus ———————————————

A FINAL CHECK OF THE LIBRARY COLLECTION

Check the following sources to be certain you have not overlooked some important, relevant information. List any additional sources that contain information you may want to use.

1. Reference Collection

2. Computer or Card Catalog

3. Periodical indexes

4. Ask the librarian to check your source log and recommend any important source you may have overlooked.

Locate the sources. If there is any information you plan to use, add the source to your source log and take notes on the additional information.

Worksheet / Activity 6–3

ACTIVITY 6-4
ORGANIZING NOTES

In this activity, students are provided with a method of organizing their notes as they prepare to write a research paper or make another type of presentation.

Time: one class period (this activity may be given as a homework assignment)

Materials: students' notes of information collected; paper and pencils

Conducted by: teacher

Activity Directions: Explain to students that they will need to organize their notes in order to plan their presentation. (See Worksheet 6-4.) Tell them: "when you are ready to organize your notes, it is important to have your focus clearly in mind. State your focus in writing." Have students think about what they intend to say in their focus.

Direct students to read through their notes on the information they have collected and to identify the main points about the focus in what has been recorded in this way: "Identify three to five main points that you want to present about your focus." (*Note:* Three to five main points are average for secondary school research assignments. You may want to suggest more for an extensive research paper.)

Have students decide on the order in which they will present the main points about the focus. Tell them: " List the main points in the order in which you plan to present them. Place the appropriate number next to the main points in your notes."

Direct students to read through their notes once again to determine the ideas and facts that are related to each main point: "Number the ideas and facts to correspond to the main points they describe."

Follow-up: You may want to review the students' notes after they have been organized with the number codes. Assist students individually if they experience difficulty.

© 1994 by Carol Collier Kuhlthau

Name _____

Date _____

Topic _____

Focus _____

STEPS IN ORGANIZING NOTES

1. Briefly state what you intend to say about your focus.

2. Read through your notes and identify three to five main points you want to present about your focus. List the main points in the order in which you plan to present them.

   I.

   II.

   III.

   IV.

   V.

   3. Read through your notes again to determine the ideas and facts that are related to each main point. Number the ideas and facts in your notes to correspond with the main points they describe.

ACTIVITY 6-5
OUTLINING

In this activity students are provided with a method for constructing an outline. The outline is a plan for presenting the findings of their library research.

Time: one class period (this activity may be given as a homework assignment)

Materials: students' notes of information collected; paper and pencils

Conducted by: teacher

Note: This activity is intended to follow activity 6-4

Activity Directions: Explain to students that an outline is a plan for presenting the findings of their library research. (See Worksheet 6-5.) Tell students "An outline is composed of a list of the topics and subtopics you intend to present. The main points you have identified in your notes and the corresponding ideas and facts make up the topics and subtopics in your outline."

Have students construct an outline by listing the main points they have identified in their notes in the order in which they plan to present them. Give these directions or something similar: "Leave ample space for adding subtopics. Read your notes and add the information that you have selected to go with each main point."

"Your outline provides the planned structure for your research presentation. You may want to add details to further guide you in preparing your presentation." The students' outlines can be as detailed as is useful to them. You may want students to include such details as what information is to be quoted, paraphrased, or summarized and their own thoughts that connect and extend the information they have collected. They may also indicate any illustrations and examples they plan to use.

Follow-up: Check each students' outline and return with suggestions for improvement. Some students may need further individual assistance in preparing the outline of a plan for presenting their research findings.

Name _____

Date _____

Topic _____

Focus _____

CONSTRUCTING AN OUTLINE

An outline is a plan for presenting the findings of your library research. List the main points in the order in which you intend to present them. Add the corresponding subpoints under each main point.

I.

    A.

    B.

    C.

    D.

II.

    A.

    B.

    C.

    D.

III.

    A.

    B.

    C.

    D.

IV.

    A.

    B.

    C.

    D.

V.

    A.

    B.

    C.

    D.

© 1994 by Carol Collier Kuhlthau

ACTIVITY 6-6
QUOTING, PARAPHRASING, AND SUMMARIZING

In this activity, students review the concepts and techniques of quoting, paraphrasing, and summarizing. They are led to plan to present their library research findings using quotations, paraphrases, and summaries.

Time: one class period (this activity may be given as a homework assignment)

Materials: students' notes of information collected; paper and pencils

Conducted by: teacher

Activity Directions: Explain to students that the information they have collected in their notes needs to be quoted, paraphrased, and summarized to present the findings of their library research. (See Worksheet 6-6.) You could explain it in this way: "Information that you plan to quote directly should have been taken down verbatim and enclosed in quotation marks. Quotations should be chosen to give the paper power and authority. You need to choose quotations carefully and use them sparingly. An overabundance of quotations diminishes their impact. Quotations should be used only when the author's wording contributes significantly to your presentation.

"Most of the information in your notes will need to be paraphrased or summarized. Paraphrasing is the complex skill of restating an author's idea in your words. Merely substituting a few words here and there is not paraphrasing. Paraphrasing requires thinking through the author's statement to comprehend it thoroughly and restating it clearly, using terms and phrases that are more familiar to you.

"You will need to summarize some of the information you have in your notes or your presentation will be too long. Summarizing involves seeing what is central to an idea and presenting it more succinctly.

"Go through your notes to identify how you plan to present the information you have collected. Mark a Q next to what you plan to quote, a P next to what you plan to paraphrase, and an S next to what you plan to summarize."

Follow-up: Offer individual help to students who experience difficulty. You may want to check students' notes to offer guidance in their decisions.

© 1994 by Carol Collier Kuhlthau

Name _____

Date _____

Topic _____

Focus _____

QUOTING, PARAPHRASING, AND SUMMARIZING

To present the findings of your library research, you will need to quote, paraphrase, and summarize the information you have collected in your notes.

1. Quoting: Quotations should be chosen to give your presentation power and authority. They should be used only when the author's wording contributes significantly to your presentation.

Mark a *Q* in your notes next to the information you plan to quote.

2. Paraphrasing: Paraphrasing is restating an author's idea in your own words. Merely substituting a few words here and there is not paraphrasing. Paraphrasing requires thinking through the author's statement to comprehend it thoroughly and restating it clearly using terms and phrases that are more familiar to you.

Mark a *P* in your notes next to the information you plan to paraphrase.

3. Summarizing: You will need to summarize some of the information you have in your notes or your presentation will be too long. Summarizing involves seeing what is central to an idea and presenting it more succinctly.

Mark an S in your notes next to the information you plan to summarize.

ACTIVITY 6-7
CONNECTING AND EXTENDING

In this activity, students review the concepts and techniques of connecting and extending. They are led to plan the connections and extensions they will use in presenting the findings of their library research.

Time: one class period (this activity may be given as a homework assignment)

Materials: students' notes of information collected

Conducted by: teacher

Activity Directions: Explain to students that in addition to presenting what they have researched in library materials they must present their own ideas through connections and extensions. (See Worksheets 1 and 2 of Activity 6-7.) You could say this: "You need to bring the separate parts into a meaningful whole. You also need to include your own ideas about your focus, which extends what you have read in library materials.

"Without connecting thoughts, a presentation is merely a group of disparate ideas and facts. The connections that you make link the ideas together. You need to decide the order in which the ideas are to be presented and to make connections tying the various points together.

"Extensions are the insights and opinions you have developed about your topic. By extending what you have researched in the library, you develop a point of view on your topic. You may include your extensions in the conclusion of your presentation.

"Consider the points you will emphasize in your presentation. State each main point and write connecting sentences leading from one main point to the next.

"Go through your notes, reading the right hand column where you have written reactions to, and extensions of, the information you have recorded. Place a check next to the comments you may want to include in your presentation. These extensions may be incorporated in the conclusion of your presentation."

Follow-up: Offer individual assistance to students who experience difficulty.

© 1994 by Carol Collier Kuhlthau

Name _____

Date _____

Topic _____

Focus _____

MAKING CONNECTIONS

Connections link the main points together. List your main points below and write a sentence to connect each main point with the next main point.

1.

2.

3.

4.

5.

Worksheet / Activity 6–7

Name _____

Date _____

Topic _____

Focus _____

DRAWING CONCLUSIONS

Read the right column of your notes where you have recorded your reactions and extensions to the information you have collected. Write a conclusion to your presentation, incorporating your interpretations. Your conclusion should correspond to your focus as stated in your introduction.

© 1994 by Carol Collier Kuhlthau

ACTIVITY 6-8
FOOTNOTES

This activity helps students learn to use footnotes to identify the sources of the information they have quoted, paraphrased, and summarized in the presentation of their research findings. They follow a recommended style manual for the correct format of footnotes or endnotes.

Time: one class period (this activity may be given as a homework assignment)

Materials: students' notes of information collected; recommended style manual

Conducted by: teacher or library media specialist

Activity Directions: Explain to students that they will need to use footnotes to identify the sources of each of the quotations they use in their research paper (See Worksheet 6-8.) and also the information they paraphrase and summarize.

You may wish to use this explanation: "Footnotes and endnotes direct the reader to your sources of information. By precisely identifying the sources you used, you can avoid plagiarism. You must be cautious not to present another author's work as your own."

Explain that there are a number of standard styles of footnotes and bibliography. Recommend one specific style manual for students to follow. (See the suggested style manuals listed in Chapter 3.) Explain to students that they must consistently use the exact format described in the style manual. Use the chalkboard to demonstrate the way to cite the most commonly used types of materials.

Have students write a draft of the footnotes for the quotation they plan to use. Check the footnotes to be certain that they comply with the style manual. Offer individual assistance to students who experience difficulty. Remind students that they must also footnote all of the information they paraphrase and summarize.

Follow-up Check the draft of the footnotes before students write their final copy. Alert them to any mistakes they have made in the citations.

Name _____

Date _____

Topic _____

Focus _____

FOOTNOTE—ROUGH DRAFT

Write footnotes for the information you plan to quote, paraphrase, and summarize. Follow the style manual recommended to you. List the footnotes below in the order in which they will appear in your presentation.

© 1994 by Carol Collier Kuhlthau

ACTIVITY 6-9
BIBLIOGRAPHY

In this activity, students list the sources they have used in a bibliography. They follow a recommended style manual for the correct form of bibliographic citation.

Time: one class period (this activity may be given as a homework assignment)

Materials: students' source logs; recommended style manual; chalkboard

Conducted by: teacher or library media specialist

Activity Directions: Remind students that they will need to list in a bibliography the sources that they have used. Explain that there are several acceptable styles of bibliography citation but that one style must be followed consistently throughout a research project. (See Worksheet 6-9.) Recommend the style they will use and refer them to the style manual: "You do not need to memorize this form of bibliography citation, but you will need to refer to the style manual for the proper form in writing the bibliography of your sources."

Describe some of the differences between footnotes and bibliography citations: "A bibliography is a list at the end of your paper of the sources you have used. Footnotes are interspersed throughout the text of your paper identifying sources as you have used them. The form of footnotes and bibliography citations are somewhat different. Page numbers must be included in footnotes but are not included in most bibliography citations. Footnotes are often abbreviated, especially when they repeat a source. In a bibliography, a source is listed once, whereas in footnotes a source is cited as many times as it was used." Compare footnotes with bibliography citations from the recommended style manual. Demonstrate the difference on a chalkboard.

Describe the variation in the form of citing different types of materials. Give examples from the style manual of the way to cite several different types of sources, such as, a single author book, a joint author book, a magazine article, an encyclopedia article, and audio-visual material.

Direct students to select the sources they will list in their bibliography from their source logs: "The citations of the sources you have listed in your source log will need to be selected and arranged to be included in the bibliography of your research paper. Rarely is every source that has been listed in your log included in the bibliography of your paper. You will need to select the sources you actually used to present the focus in your research paper."

Have students arrange the sources alphabetically by numbering the selected sources in the order in which they will appear in the bibliography and then by compiling a list according to the numbers assigned to each item.

Follow-up: Check the draft of the bibliography before students write their final copy. Alert them to any mistakes they may have made in the citations.

Name _____

Date _____

Topic _____

Focus _____

BIBLIOGRAPHY—ROUGH DRAFT

Select the sources you used from those listed in your source log. List the sources below in alphabetical order. Follow the style manual for the recommended form of bibliography citations.

© 1994 by Carol Collier Kuhlthau

STAGES OF THE
LIBRARY RESEARCH PROCESS:

Section 7
Assessing the Process

TASK	To evaluate the library research process.
THOUGHTS	Increase self-awareness • Identify problems and successes • Plan research strategy for future assignments.
FEELINGS	Sense of accomplishment or sense of disappointment.
ACTIONS	Seek evidence of focus • Assess use of time • Evaluate use of sources • Reflect on use of librarian.
STRATEGIES	Draw time line • Make flow chart • Discuss with teacher and library media specialist • Write summary statement.

SECTION 7

Assessing the Process

TASK OF THE SEVENTH STAGE

The final task of students in the research process is to evaluate what they have done. They need to review their progress throughout the research process to identify what caused them difficulty and to determine what they might do differently to improve their process as well as the presentation of their findings.

The purpose of evaluation is to identify what learning has taken place and where further instruction and practice are needed. The traditional assessment of a research assignment is the teacher's evaluation of the research paper or other form of presenting the findings of library research. A grade on a research paper is a limited indication of the specific learning that has taken place in the research activities or of the further instructional needs of students. Evaluation of the end product of library research rarely identifies specific weaknesses and strengths in the library research process of students.

Self-assessment of the research activities can enable students to pinpoint particular problems and can lead to improvement and new learning. Self-evaluation, of course, does not take the place of the teacher's evaluation. Students' assessment of their own research activities and the teacher's evaluation of the product of library research go hand-in-hand to help students improve their research process

Evaluation should take place immediately following the completion of the research assignment. The entire process should be fresh in students' minds when they reflect on their progress. Prompt feedback is an essential component of learning. Self-assessment and the teacher's evaluation should be planned as the last stage of the library research process.

Students need to be introduced to strategies and techniques that reveal the research process for examination. This program offers a number of ways to assist students in assessing their library research process.

Feelings of Students After the Research Process

When students look back over their library research, they often experience either a feeling of accomplishment or a sense of disappointment. If they have been able to locate and present information on their focus in a way that meets the requirements of the assignment, they usually feel satisfied. Some students will be

172

pleasantly surprised at the results they have been able to produce. Many will want to talk about their research projects, enthusiastically explaining their focus and the findings of their library research.

Students experience a sense of disappointment when their expectations of the results of their library research have not been met. These students frequently have not identified a focus during the research process and have not been successful in supporting or presenting a focus in their research paper.

Students need to become aware of their feelings at the end of the library research process. They should attempt to identify the reason for their feelings of accomplishment or disappointment. Their feelings are often an indication of how successful they have been in meeting the requirements of the research assignment. As they have more experience with library research and come to understand their own process, their feelings at the completion of a research assignment become a more reliable indicator in assessing the success of their library research.

Increasing Self-Awareness

Self-awareness can lead students to view themselves more objectively. When they become more objective in assessing their progress in library research, they are better prepared to learn from their mistakes and successes. They need to be objective in assessing their own research activities. This book's program has been planned to make students more aware of their process while they are moving through the stages of a library assignment.

Assisting students to reflect on their experience in working on a research assignment helps to reveal their research process to them. Students are often surprised when they discover the various stages they have come through. One student described discovering stages in the research process in this way: "Well, I guess there are three phases. . . . I never realized that I did this. I never realized I did all the work in three phases. I just thought I did all of the work the last minute and did my report."

Once students are aware of having experienced stages in the library research process, they are able to plan their library research activities accordingly. Their approach to library research becomes more realistic, efficient, and effective. They begin to build their thoughts on their topics within the various stages of the library research process.

There are four elements in the research process that students need to become more aware of in their assessment at the end of a research assignment. The elements are the evidence of a focus, use of time, use of sources, and use of the library media specialist. An awareness of their use of these elements in library research can enable students to improve their approach to future research assignments.

Evidence of a Focus

After a research assignment has been completed, students should assess the presentations of their library research findings for the evidence of a focus. The focus of the research paper should be clearly stated in the introduction and supported in the body of the paper with the facts and ideas collected from library sources.

Many students' research papers lack a clear focus. As one student described it, "I had a general idea but not a specific focus. . . . As I was writing I didn't know what my focus was. When I finished, I didn't know what my focus was. . . . I don't think I ever acquired a focus. It was an impossible paper to write." Students need to become aware of the difference that a focus makes in a research paper. They can learn to identify a focus early in the research process.

Students should be able to express their focus clearly and succinctly at the end of a research assignment. A fairly accurate test of the presence of a focus is being able to state the focus after the assignment has been completed. Students with unfocused papers tend to name the general topic when asked to tell what their paper was about. When asked to describe the focus of his paper, one student stated, "I don't know. I did have one. It had to do with transcendentalism and the essay on self-reliance more than anything else. . . . I guess it was transcendental-ism and Emerson." Another student had similar difficulty stating the focus of her paper. "It was just Fitzgerald and his books." Students who have a clearly identified and supported focus tend to state the focus of their paper rather than the general topic. One student clearly described the focus of her paper, "I decided to show how the place itself (Brook Farm) helped the people to use the ideas of transcendentalism to make the community work."

By assessing the presence of a focus in their papers, students learn the function of a focus. They become more aware of the mistakes they made in presenting the focus as well as the success they had in supporting the focus. In this way, they learn the importance of forming a focus early in the research process, which they can develop and support through the information they collect from library sources.

Use of Time

An important element in the assessment of the research process of students is how they paced themselves in their library research. Students need to become aware of the way they use their time in a research assignment. The best time for students to consider the research process as a whole and assess their use of time is shortly after the assignment has been completed.

Many students think that they procrastinated until shortly before the assignment was due and then they did all of their research in a short span of time. However, when they reflect on what has actually taken place in the early stages of the research process, they are often surprised to find that rather than procrastinating, they were thinking and learning about their topic in a general way.

As students assess their pace in a research assignment, they become aware of the stages they have progressed through to develop their research presenta-tion. The student who explained that he had not realized that he did all of the work in three phases, but thought that he put it off until the last minute, was becoming aware of different stages in the library research process. By assessing their research activities, students can become aware that at the beginning their thoughts about their topic are developing. Next, they are exploring for a focus and finally they are collecting information pertaining to their focus. As students assess their use of time in a research assignment, they can learn to pace themselves effectively in future library research.

Use of Sources

The way the sources in the library collection have been used is an important consideration in assessing students' library research. At the completion of a research assignment, students should recall the order in which they used sources. Were the sources used randomly or were sources used in a logical sequence?

Students can become aware of the sequence in which they used library sources. Using general sources first and working toward the more specific sources matches the stages of the research process. At the beginning of the process, general sources help students to learn about the topic. As they explore for a focus, sources on various aspects of the topic need to be used. After a focus has been formed, information must be collected from sources with specific information about the focus. Students can learn to develop patterns of use that proceed from general to specific sources.

One student described discovering the use of sources in this way: "The ones [sources] in the middle are most useful because in the beginning you're not definitely sure what you are doing. Then as you get direction toward the middle, you know what you are looking for. In the end you are just looking for extra things so you are sure you have everything, but a lot of it is repeat."

Students can become familiar with different ways to use sources in the various stages of the research process. For example, the library catalog can be used in each stage of the process at a different level and for a different purpose. It is important for students to become aware of the intricacies of using library sources and indexes and to become more proficient at using sources for a variety of purposes. They need to reflect on their research activities to assess their use of library sources through the different stages of the process.

Use of the Library Media Specialist

In assessing their research activities, students need to reflect on their use of the library media specialist. Students' expectations of how a librarian might help them are often either too high or too low. Some students expect a librarian to produce the sources that are the key to their library research assignment immediately. Others avoid asking for help and attempt to be totally independent in their library research. They need to become aware that neither extreme fosters the best use of the library media specialist.

Students can review the stages of their research process and analyze their use of the librarian at each stage. As they recall the problems that they encountered, they should consider how the librarian might have helped them. They can become aware of the different levels of information need at the various stages in the research process and can assess their requests for information at each stage. They can learn how to ask for information and to practice stating requests that enable the librarian to be helpful to them. Here is how one student described her inability to use library sources as a result of a reluctance to seek the assistance of a librarian: "I went to the university library and I really didn't get anything out of that because it was so huge that I didn't know where anything was."

Students can learn to use the librarian as one of the resources in the library. They must learn not to be overly demanding by asking for information that they can readily locate themselves. On the other hand, they need to think of the librarian as an access point to the collection and an expert on library research. Interaction with the librarian is part of the library research process and students can learn when and how to request information from the librarian.

Techniques for Assessing the Research Process

The library research process is an individual endeavor that is difficult for students or teachers to assess without some ways of exposing it for observation. A number of techniques for helping students observe their research process are offered in this book. Each of these techniques reveals the research process to enable students to become more aware of their own progress through the stages, to identify problems, and to take steps toward improvement. The activities offered in this chapter, construction of a time line and a flow chart, and conferences and writing, are ways of reviewing the research activities for assessment.

Time Line

Throughout this program, the time line of the research process has been used to help students visualize the stages in the process and to identify where they are in the process as they proceed through the stages. When students have completed the research assignment, they can personalize the time line by drawing one for their own research process.

By drawing a line across a piece of paper and identifying the initiation of the assignment at the far left and the completion of the presentation at the far right, students have a blank time line on which to reveal their research process. They can refer to their journals to recall events and dates to be placed on their time lines. Their time lines should show when they chose their topic, when they explored for their focus, when they formed their focus, when they collected information, when they completed their library research, and when they prepared their presentation.

This technique reveals to students the stages in their own library research process. In this way, they can assess their use of time during the stages of their research. When stages of the library research process become apparent to students, they are able to plan better use of their time in future research assignments.

Flow Chart

The flow chart, like the time line, reveals the entire research process to students. The flow chart, however, is not confined to the stages of the research process but includes additional details of the students' library research.

Students are given a piece of paper with one box in the upper left corner and another box in the lower right corner. The first box is labeled "received assignment" and the other box is labeled "wrote paper." Students make a flow chart of connecting boxes to show how they progressed through the library research process. Each connecting box reveals a step they took to complete their library research assignment. Students can use their journals to help them recall the progress of their research.

On the flow chart, students can show when they used the library, what sources they located, how their thoughts about their topic evolved into a focus, and the steps they took in collecting information. The chart depicts a detailed analysis of the library research process from beginning to end.

Constructing a flow chart gives students an overview of their research activities. They can readily visualize the library research process as a whole when it is charted on one sheet of paper. This overview offers students a way to assess their progress and to identify problem spots. They can begin to analyze the steps they took and determine what they might do differently the next time they are assigned library research or when they research something on their own.

Conferences

Conferences with the teacher or the librarian at the completion of the research assignment are extremely effective for helping students to recall and assess their own research activities. By using such techniques as the time line and the flow chart, students can describe their library research. In this way, stages and steps in the library research process that are commonly overlooked or ignored can be examined and evaluated. The teacher or librarian can offer specific recommendations for improving the library research.

Students benefit from the one-to-one guidance offered in a conference. Conferences do take considerable time, but for new researchers the rewards can be substantial. When students talk about their library research process with the teacher or the librarian using the recommended devices to reveal the various steps and stages, learning often takes place that is both lasting and transferable.

Writing a Summary Statement

Students' ability to write about their focus after the research assignment is completed is a good way to assess the presence of a focus in their research. If they have identified and presented a clear focus, they are likely to be able to write about the focus in a brief summary statement. On the other hand, if their presentation was unfocused, they are likely to have difficulty stating a focus.

By writing a summary paragraph to explain the findings of their library research, students become more aware of their focus or lack of focus. They begin to understand how a focus affects their thinking about a topic. Being able to express succinctly what their research was about is evidence that a focus was present. Students who are aware of the function of a focus are apt to seek one in future library research. A clear focus enables them to make a summary statement about their topic.

Role of the Teacher

An essential element in teaching is evaluating learning. The teacher, as an experienced evaluator, plays a significant role in helping students assess their own library research process. Students need guidance in viewing their library research to determine their successes and weaknesses.

By using techniques recommended in this book, teachers can help students assess their own library research activities. Holding individual conferences to discuss a student's time line or to help a student construct a flow chart are excellent ways to reveal the library research process for evaluation and for identifying particular problems and strengths. Students need guidance in examining how they used their time in the library research activities. They need assistance in examining how they developed and supported their focus. Teachers can guide secondary students to visualize their own library research process and to identify problem areas needing attention.

Role of the Library Media Specialist

Library media specialists should be involved in the assessment of the research process. As experts on library research activities, as well as the sources in the library collection, they can help students identify problems and recommend strategies for improvement.

Students need help to view the library as a whole and to assess their use of sources in relation to the variety of sources available. Library media specialists can introduce sources that might have been used but were not. Students also need help in identifying times in their library research when the librarian might have been helpful and been turned to as a resource.

The roles of the teacher and the library media specialist overlap somewhat in helping students to assess their library research process. They work as a team to guide self-evaluation. It is important that they share responsibility in offering students conferences and other strategies for students' assessment of their own library research process.

The following activities assist students in assessing their library research process.

ACTIVITY 7-1
A PERSONALIZED TIME LINE

In this activity students draw a time line of their own research process. The time line helps them recall how they used their time during the stages of their process, to identify problems, and to plan to make better use of their time in future research assignments.

Time: one class period

Materials: journals; chalkboard

Conducted by: teacher or library media specialist

Activity Directions: Explain to students that they are going to draw a time line of their own research process. (See Worksheet 7-1.) Demonstrate on a chalkboard as you give the following directions: "Draw a line horizontally across a piece of paper. At the beginning of the line on the left, write 'received assignment.' At the end of the line on the right, write 'completed presentation.'"

Have the students record the following on their time lines:
1. when they chose their topic
2. when they explored for a focus
3. when they formed a focus
4. when they collected information
5. when they completed their library research
6. when they prepared their presentation

Recommend that students refer to their journals to recall events and dates to be placed on their time line. Show some time lines that other students have drawn. (See Figures 7-1 through 7-4 for examples.)

When students have completed drawing their time lines, ask them to consider how they used their time in the research process.

Variation: After they have drawn their time lines, have students write a paragraph on how they used their time and what they might want to do differently in future research assignments.

Follow-up: see Activity 7-3.

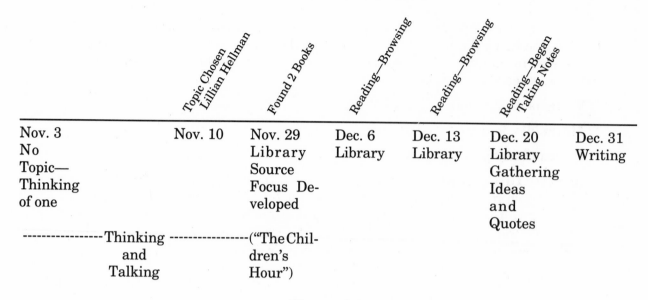

	Topic Chosen Lillian Hellman	Found 2 Books	Reading—Browsing	Reading—Browsing	Reading—Began Taking Notes	
Nov. 3 No Topic— Thinking of one	Nov. 10	Nov. 29 Library Source Focus Developed	Dec. 6 Library	Dec. 13 Library	Dec. 20 Library Gathering Ideas and Quotes	Dec. 31 Writing
----------------Thinking and Talking		----------------("The Children's Hour")				

Figure 7-1

Nov. 4 Pick Topic Took Out Some Books	Nov. 5 Ency.	Nov. 6 Literary Criticism	Nov. 9 Dec. 9 Jan. 1 ——————— Research Picked Basis of Paper "Recurrent" Themes	Jan. 2 Started Writing	Jan. 3 Finish Writing	Jan. 4 Paper Due

Figure 7-2

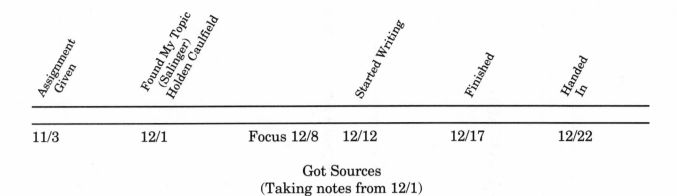

| 11/3 | 12/1 | Focus 12/8 | 12/12 | 12/17 | 12/22 |

Got Sources
(Taking notes from 12/1)

Figure 7-3

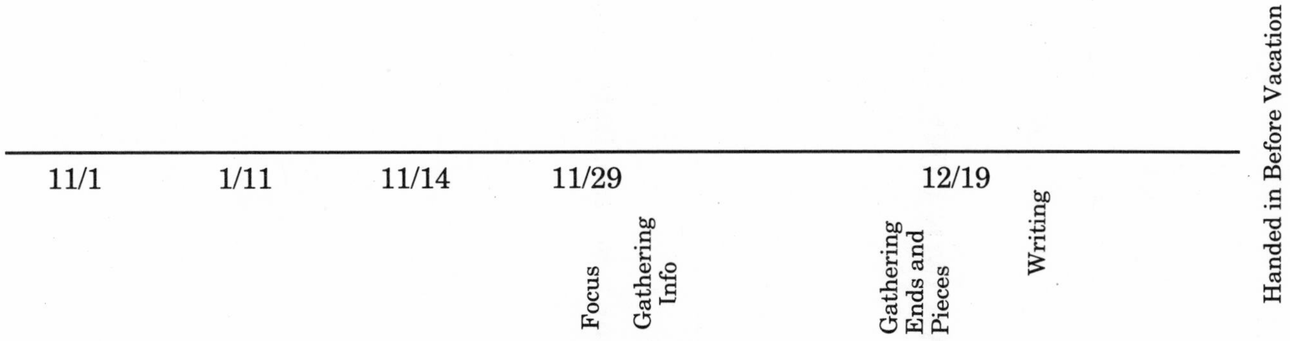

| 11/1 | 1/11 | 11/14 | 11/29 | | 12/19 | |

Figure 7-4

Name _____

Date _____

MAKING A TIME LINE OF YOUR RESEARCH PROCESS

received
assignment

completed
presentation

Record the following events on your time line. Date each event and add any details you want to include to describe your research process.

1. Selected topic

2. Explored for focus

3. Formed focus

4. Collected information

5. Completed library research

6. Prepared presentation

© 1994 by Carol Collier Kuhlthau

ACTIVITY 7-2
FLOW CHART

Constructing a flow chart gives students a visual overview of how they conducted themselves through their research process. The flow chart is more detailed than the time line. Students can more readily visualize the process as a whole when it is charted on one piece of paper. This overview offers students a way to assess their progress and to identify problems.

Time: one class period

Materials: journals; chalkboard

Conducted by: teacher or library media specialist

Note: Many secondary students have learned the techniques of flow charting in mathematics. Those students who are unfamiliar with flow charting will probably need a preliminary introduction prior to this activity.

Activity Directions: Announce to students that they are going to make a flow chart of their research process. (See Worksheet 7-2.) You may wish to use this statement: "The flow chart will give you an overview of your research process. This overview will help you assess your progress and identify problem spots."

As you give the following directions, demonstrate on a chalkboard: "Draw one box in the upper left corner of your paper and another box in the lower right corner of your paper. In the first box write 'received assignment.' In the other box, write 'completed presentation.'"

"Make a flow chart by connecting boxes to show how you progressed through the research process. Each connecting box reveals a step you took to complete your library research assignment. Use your journal to help you recall the progress of your research." Show some flow charts that other students have made. (See Figures 7-5 and 7-6.)

Suggest that students show the following on their flow charts:

1. when they used a library
2. sources they located
3. usefulness of sources
4. thoughts about their topic
5. development of a focus
6. steps toward collecting information
7. when they completed their research

When students have completed their flow charts, ask them to identify problem spots and to consider what they might do to improve their process in future research assignments.

Variation: After students have completed their flow charts, have them write a paragraph assessing their research activities, identifying problems and how they might improve their process.

Follow-up: see Activity 7-3.

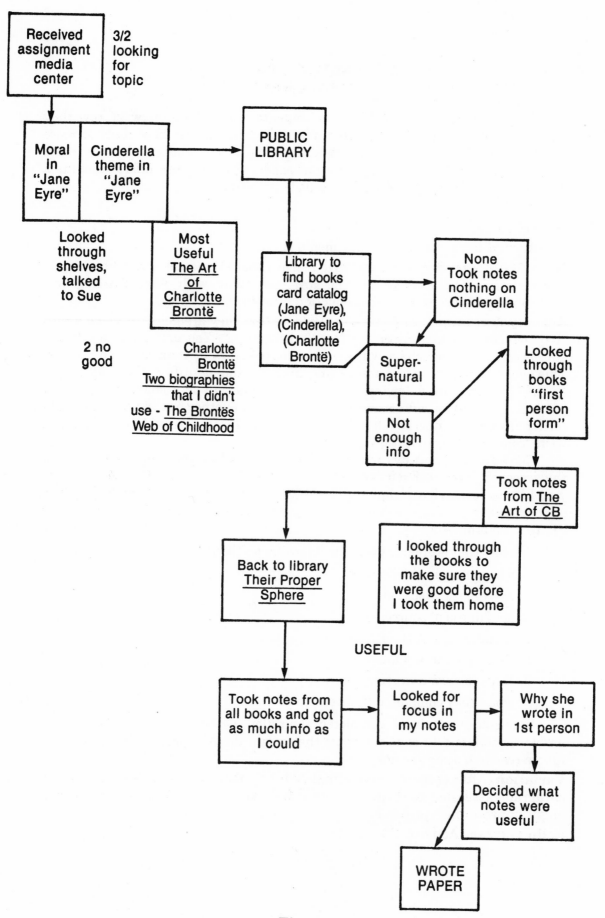

Figure 7–5

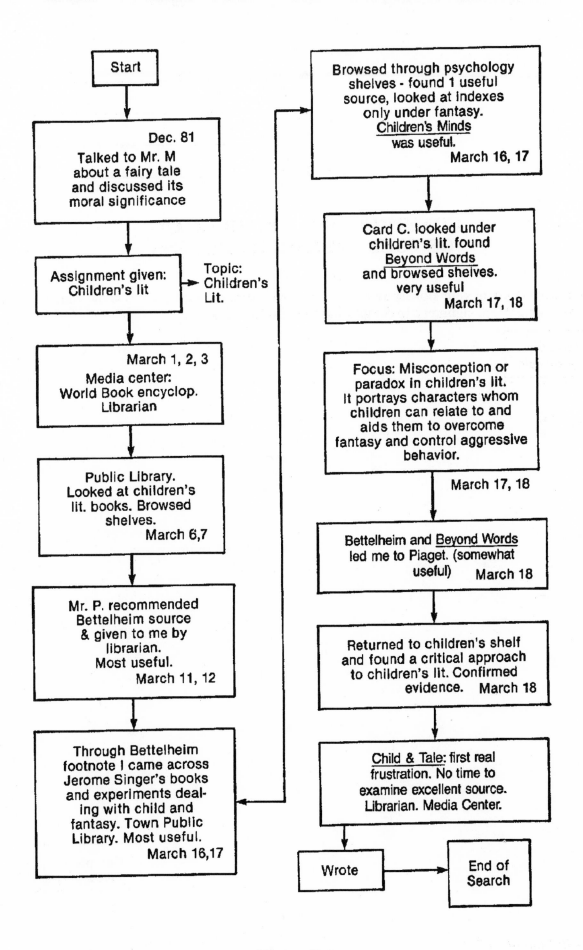

Start

Dec. 81

Talked to Mr. M about a fairy tale and discussed its moral significance

Assignment given: Children's lit → Topic: Children's Lit.

March 1, 2, 3

Media center: World Book encyclop. Librarian

Public Library. Looked at children's lit. books. Browsed shelves.

March 6,7

Mr. P. recommended Bettelheim source & given to me by librarian. Most useful.

March 11, 12

Through Bettelheim footnote I came across Jerome Singer's books and experiments dealing with child and fantasy. Town Public Library. Most useful.

March 16,17

Browsed through psychology shelves - found 1 useful source, looked at indexes only under fantasy. <u>Children's Minds</u> was useful.

March 16, 17

Card C. looked under children's lit. found <u>Beyond Words</u> and browsed shelves. very useful

March 17, 18

Focus: Misconception or paradox in children's lit. It portrays characters whom children can relate to and aids them to overcome fantasy and control aggressive behavior.

March 17, 18

Bettelheim and <u>Beyond Words</u> led me to Piaget. (somewhat useful)   March 18

Returned to children's shelf and found a critical approach to children's lit. Confirmed evidence.   March 18

<u>Child & Tale</u>: first real frustration. No time to examine excellent source. Librarian. Media Center.

Wrote → **End of Search**

Figure 7–6

Name _____

Date _____

Topic _____

Focus _____

CONSTRUCTING A FLOW CHART
OF YOUR RESEARCH PROCESS

Make a flow chart of your library research process by connecting boxes to show your progress from receiving the assignment to completing the presentation.

Received
Assignment

© 1994 by Carol Collier Kuhlthau

Completed
Presentation

Activity / Worksheet 7–2

ACTIVITY 7-3
CONFERENCES

Conferences help students recall and assess their own research process. Students use their time lines and their flow charts to describe their process. In this way, stages and techniques that are commonly overlooked can be assessed and recommendations for improvement can be made.

Time: 10 to 15 minutes with each student

Materials: personalized time lines (see Activity 7-1); flow charts (see Activity 7-2)

Conducted by: teacher and library media specialist

Activity Directions: Meet with each student individually. Distribute copies of Worksheet 7-3 in advance of the conferences. Ask the student to describe his or her research process by using first the time line and then the flow chart. Using the time line, help student visualize the stages of the research process and assess his or her use of time during the process. Using the flow chart, have the student describe how sources of information were located and which sources were most useful. Also ask students to explain how librarians were a part of their process.

Have the student describe the development of his or her focus on both the time line and the flow chart. Recommend steps and techniques to improve the student's research process.

Variation: In a class discussion, have students share their experiences in the research process as revealed on their time lines and flow charts.

Name _____

Date _____

Topic _____

Focus _____

PREPARING FOR A CONFERENCE

A. Using the time line of your research process, be able to describe:

1. your progress through the stages of the research process

2. how you used your time in the research activities

B. Using the flow chart of your research process, be able to describe:

1. how you located information and which sources were most useful

2. how your focus evolved from the information you located

© 1994 by Carol Collier Kuhlthau

ACTIVITY 7-4
WRITING A SUMMARY STATEMENT

Students' ability to write about their focus after the research assignment is completed is a good way to assess the presence of a focus in their research. By writing a summary paragraph to describe the findings of their library research, students become aware of their focus or lack of focus.

Time: 20 minutes

Materials: paper and pencils

Conducted by: teacher

Activity Directions: Distribute paper (or Worksheet 7-4) and have students write a brief summary of the findings of their library research. Ask them "What was the central idea in your library research findings?" Allow students 10 to 15 minutes for writing.

Collect the writings and read for evidence of a focus. Assist students individually where the writing lacks a focus.

Variation: Have each student share his or her writing with the class. Discuss the presence of a focus in each student's writing. Small discussion groups may also be used for this purpose. Divide the class into groups of four or five students. Have each student read his or her summary and then have the group discuss evidence of a focus.

© 1994 by Carol Collier Kuhlthau

Name _____

Date _____

Topic _____

Focus _____

A SUMMARY STATEMENT

Write a brief summary of the findings of your library research. Describe the central idea or focus of your presentation.